THE
SYNAGOG

IN HISTORY AND ARCHITECTURE

MEIR BEN-DOV

THE GOLDEN AGE: SYNAGOGUES OF SPAIN IN HISTORY AND ARCHITECTURE

MEIR BEN-DOV

URIM PUBLICATIONS
Jerusalem • New York

In memory of my uncle and aunt
Avraham Ben-Dov, 1876–1951
and his wife, Rachel (née Abarbanel), 1876–1950

The Golden Age: Synagogues of Spain in History and Architecture
By Meir Ben-Dov

Translation from Hebrew by Shmuel Himelstein.

Printed in Israel. First Edition.
Hardcover edition ISBN 13: 978-965-524-0160
Paperback edition ISBN 13: 978-965-524-0184
Urim Publications
P.O. Box 52287, Jerusalem 91521 Israel

Lambda Publishers Inc.
527 Empire Blvd., Brooklyn, NY 11225 USA
Tel: 718-972-5449 Fax: 718-972-6307, mh@ejudaica.com

www.UrimPublications.com

The English edition of this book has been published
with the kind assistance of

Edgar Astaire

in memory of his parents

Max-Mordechai and Esther Astaire

Edgar Astaire felt that visitors to Spain
would be given a new dimension
on the country's Jewish history.

Contents

Preface

he heritage of Spanish Jewry covers many areas. There is no corner, nor even the tiniest recess, in the realm of its culture that has not been the subject of research – the *halakhah* literature with all its components, ethical writings, sacred and secular poetry, *piyyut* and prayer. There is also considerable literature on the Hebrew language, grammar, and general philosophy of Spanish Jewry. The different realms of the physical sciences were studied by the great scholars of the Jewish culture of the Golden Age of Spain – architecture, oceanography, astronomy, mathematics, physics and, of course, medicine. The Jewish scholars of that era had access to all the arts as well: painting, sculpture, poetry, and music. Names such as Alfasi, Maimonides, Nahmanides, Dunash ibn Labrat. Bahya ibn Pakuda, Alharizi, Yehudah Halevi, Ibn Gevirol, and dozens and even hundreds of others are evidence of a flourishing era such as the Jewish people had never before witnessed.

It is to only be expected that modern-day scholars – both Jewish and non-Jewish – have found fertile ground for studies in the different branches of Jewish culture in Spain. If we mention only a few of the scholars of the last few generations, we will be able to understand to what an extent the Spanish tradition has become an accepted field of study. Sherman, in his monumental work on the poetry of Spain; Yitzhak Baer, Eliyahu Ashtor, and Alfredo Mordekhai Rabilo in their excellent studies on the history of the Jews of Spain; Haim Beinart in his detailed investigation of the history of the Jews just prior to their expulsion and afterward under the Inquisition; and Contra-Burgos and Mays in their study of the synagogues in Spain and Hebrew inscriptions, are the authors of some of the basic studies regarding the Spanish tradition. We must also mention those who preceded them – Heinrich Graetz, Simon Dubnow, and Salo Wittmayer Baron – and many others, all of whom laid the foundations of research in this area.

Since there is still room for a great deal of research in several fields, including the architecture of the synagogues of Spanish Jewry, I have elected to shed some light on this dark corner. However, I have not gone into detail about the culture of Spanish Jewry. There was no reason to do so, both because of space limitations and because scholars have researched this area thoroughly.

Nevertheless, I have written a brief preface that deals with the roots and traditions of Spanish Jewry. I have done so because of the novel approach I adopted regarding the part played by the Jews of the Land of Israel in determining the culture of Spanish Jewry. A study on this topic will be published separately. Toward the end of the Byzantine era a major and comprehensive culture developed in the Land of Israel that was transferred, along with its leading lights, to Spain during the first decades of Muslim rule. In Spain it found fertile ground for the era that became known as the Golden Age. The Jews of the Land of Israel of that time were involved in the architecture of Jewish places of worship and built many synagogues in the country. The remains of dozens of such synagogues have been discovered there, and others continue to be discovered. It would appear that the architectural traditions of the Land of Israel influenced the synagogues built in the Diaspora, especially for Jews who left the Land of Israel and carried its roots and traditions with them.

Although conditions outside the country, which was under an oppressive foreign regime, brought about changes in the architectural perceptions of the Jews, they drew inspiration from the new cultures with which they came into contact in Spain – first Arab culture and then Christian-Arabic culture. Still, one cannot speak of the synagogues in Spain without considering their sources, which trace back to the Land of Israel.

Even though this architectural study is so far the largest in its field, it is only the first attempt of this kind. The study of synagogues in Spain awaits others who will carry it further.

Author's Note

In 1992, the Jewish world marked the five-hundredth anniversary of the expulsion of the Jews from Spain, which most Jews living there had considered a second homeland. The Jews were terribly disappointed in the country and in its rulers, who owed their progress and advancement to the highest levels in all areas of life – political, economic, military, agricultural, architectural and, of course, commercial – to the Jewish communities that had lived there for hundreds of years. During that year, Spain also marked the date of the unforgettable and courageous voyage of Christopher Columbus, which led to the discovery of the New World – America.

The expulsion was accompanied by cruelty, physical and mental torture and by theft of property. But the vast majority of the Jews, leaders and commoners alike, steadfastly preserved the values of their faith, tradition and pride with honor and devotion.

Some good came out of the pain, however, since with the expulsion from Spain and the scattering of the Jews throughout the known world – eastward to Babylon, Palestine and Turkey and westward to the Netherlands, Germany and even Poland – the Jewish communities there gained strength and their culture thrived.

One of the most important fields of Jewish activity in Spain was religious architecture: the building of synagogues. The architects and builders alike were Jews. Thousands of synagogues existed in Spain at the time. Some were magnificent and large, while others served communities and families. The architecture of the synagogues in Spain, with the same Jewish heritage as its background, was a vital component in the history of Jewish architecture.

The Jews brought the flavor of the synagogue architecture that they had known in Spain to the places of their dispersion.

These and other subjects are dealt with in this book, the result of years of architectural research of synagogues in Spain itself and in the lands of its cultural heritage.

Meir Ben-Dov

Introduction

lthough my involvement in the study of the architecture of the synagogues in Spain began by chance, it eventually became a book that I could not put down. In 1970, I went to Spain for the first time on a study trip. I had two goals: to see and hear from a primary source about the preservation and reconstruction of ancient archaeological and historical sites, areas in which the Spanish authorities had taken modest but significant steps. My second aim, of no less importance, was to study and observe the Muslim architecture of palaces and mosques. For a Jew, a tour of Spain cannot help but include the few Jewish sites that still survive, which are silent echoes of the Golden Age of Spain. The feelings we have carried in our hearts ever since the horrors of the Inquisition and the expulsion of the Jews from Spain, cannot but emerge when a Jew treads upon Spanish soil. One continually hears echoes of those terrible times, which marked the end of one of the most important eras in Jewish history, in one's mind. These echoes grow louder when one visits the synagogues in Toledo or Cordoba. To me, this confrontation with the past was totally unexpected. Since I could recollect no extensive study of these impressive buildings, I was amazed that they were still standing.

When I returned to Israel, I began to search for anything I could find about those buildings, and especially architectural studies, these being my primary interest. I soon realized that very little work has been done in this area. Although there are exceptional studies of Spanish Jewry, such as Yitzhak Baer's *History of the Jews in Christian Spain* and Eliyahu Ashtori's study of Jewish communities under Islamic rule, they deal with history rather than architecture. I finally found a study of the synagogues of Spain that was published in 1956 in Spanish, called *The Spanish Synagogues* by Francisco Cantera Burgos, one of the greatest scholars of Spanish Jewry and the director of the faculty of Jewish studies at the University of Madrid at the time.

However, even though this work is a cornerstone in the study of the synagogues in Spain and deals with Jewish inscriptions in these synagogues, it hardly deals with the synagogues' architecture. The little material mentioned there relates to the primary studies of the Spanish architect Czekelius.

Although I found fragmentary comments about the architecture of the Spanish synagogues in the Hebrew literature, they were all based on secondary sources. I learned that an Israeli scholar of the architecture of medieval synagogues, Jacob Pinkerfeld, had planned to visit Spain and to investigate the architecture of its synagogues. His research in Italy, North Africa, and the Land of Israel guaranteed that this would be a serious and important study. But Pinkerfeld could not complete his mission. In 1956 he was shot to death by soldiers of the Arab Legion during an archaeological convention at Ramat Rahel. I therefore decided to make time between semesters to investigate the architecture of the synagogues in Spain.

At least five of my many trips to Spain since then have been in order to investigate the synagogues and their architecture. At the same time, I also investigated the history of the Jews in Spain and proposed new ideas regarding the origins of this remarkable community in its Golden Age, and I share my conclusions in the first chapter of this book.

This is how I did my work: I visited Spain a number of times, traveled to various synagogues, studied in each place, measured, prepared sketches and took photographs. I completed each study once I returned to Israel. The results of my work are in the book that you are holding.

I hope that this study will serve as a small brick in a large structure that still awaits one who will do justice to the study of the architecture of Jewish synagogues throughout the world.

I have also included studies of three Spanish synagogues in our region. The first is a study of the synagogue in Fostat, Egypt. This synagogue is the most ancient functioning synagogue that exists today. The second, about the Nahmanides synagogue in Jerusalem, includes a new proposal abuot its identity resulting from my studies regarding Jerusalem's past. The innovation in my proposal and its links to the Spanish architecture and to an existing building which was converted to a synagogue make it an appropriate field of study in the present work. The third is a study of the synagogue in the town of Aley in Lebanon, a building on the verge of collapse. Even though it was built only approximately ninety years ago, it shows the influence of the Spanish synagogues. Thus, these three studies complement the work of this volume.

I would like to thank those who helped me to publish this study. When I flew to Spain, I took with me a warm letter of endorsement from the Spanish consul of East Jerusalem of that time, my friend Mr. Jose Antonio Ramacho, whom I met during tours of the digs on the Temple Mount and in the Old City of Jerusalem. In most cases, this letter opened various doors for me among priests and monks and also enabled me to measure and photograph various synagogues without interference. However, although the letter was ornate, befitting a letter of appointment from the Middle Ages, it did not always help. Several times I was astonished at the scorn with which some Spanish civil servants treated the letter of their official representative in Jerusalem. In any event, Jose Antonio Ramacho has my heartfelt appreciation and thanks.

I would also like to thank Mr. Edgar Astaire, a Jewish resident of London, who donated a sum that enabled me to fly to Spain and stay there during one of the five times I traveled to Spain for the purposes of this study.

Thanks also to David Davidowitz, an engineer who has studied synagogues in Poland, and to the collector and scholar Yitzhak Einhorn, from whom I borrowed books relating to this study. I would also like to thank Ms. Malka Levi, Ms. Sarah Karni, and Mr. Yitzhak Yaakobi, all of whom contributed in various ways to the publication of this book. I do not believe that the editing of this volume, including bringing it to its conclusion, would have been possible without the help of my family: my wife Tzippy and our children Eran, Guy, and Yuval. They bore the brunt of the study, which was carried out during my free time and therefore stole from theirs. The assistance I received from them was invaluable.

Most of the photographs in this book were taken by me. Some of the photographs appear here through the kind permission of the Spanish Ministry of Education and Ministry of Tourism, for which I thank them. The final sketches, as they appear in the book, are the products of the gifted hands of Ms. Martha Ritmayer, a volunteer who came from Holland to work on the Temple Mount and found her place at the drawing board. Her talent, ability, and desire have made her one of the best architectural sketchers in the fields of archaeological and architectural drawing in Israel today. Martha was blessed not only with talented hands but also with the ability to learn and analyze buildings. We worked together on the sketches that I brought with me, and the result is the excellent sketches that the reader will see. My deepest thanks to Martha for that.

The original publication of this book in Hebrew was undertaken by the Dvir Publishing House, whose owner and professional staff did everything possible to have the book appear in the most aesthetic manner. My thanks to all of them.

I would also like to thank Amnon Sasson, the Hebrew language editor, and Steven Lobel, the designer of the book.

I dedicate this book to the memory of my uncle, Avraham Ben-Dov, and his wife Rahel, of the Abarbanel family, members of the Second Aliyah who immigrated to Palestine from Russia in 1906 and died in Tel Aviv in 1951. They had no children.

Abraham Ben-Dov (Kossakowski), my father's older brother, who was born in the town of Vinitza in the Podolia district of the Ukraine, was one of the town's notables. He was involved in theater reviews in the Russian press, and at the same time was one of the active members of the town's Jewish defense force, participating in organizing active defense during the pogroms by the Ukrainian rioters. His brother, my uncle Yaakov, was killed during one of those pogroms as he stood guard, and Abraham himself was sentenced to prison for his activities. In 1905 he was chosen to represent his town as a delegate of the Seventh Jewish Congress in Basel. Immediately afterwards he immigrated to Palestine, following his girlfriend, who later his wife.

Rachel, of the Abarbanel family, was the secretary of the poet Hayyim Nahman Bialik in Odessa. Although the poet urged her repeatedly to stay, she decided to follow her Zionist conscience and immigrated to Palestine. In order to support herself and to be useful in the new society that was being formed, she studied midwifery and eventually found work in Metulla. My uncle Abraham followed her and they were married there.

Filled with the ideals of equality, comradeship and Zionism, they founded a communal store in Metulla that was the first cooperative in Palestine. The farmers were unable to resist the temptation of making purchases with payments stretched for over a year, and during a year of famine they were unable to pay their bills. Thus my uncle and aunt lost their money and moved to Tel Aviv, where they were among its first residents and where they remained for the rest of their lives. They were devoted Zionists. May this book be a memorial to them.

Meir Ben-Dov
Jerusalem

Chapter 1 The Origins and Heritage of Spanish Jewry: The Golden Age

he greatest era of Spanish Jewry, the Golden Age of Spain, reached its peak from the tenth through the twelfth centuries C.E. Throughout the past two thousand years, in its various dispersions, the Jewish people saw no better times than those in Spain during its Golden Age. During this time the Jews flourished economically, politically, socially, and especially culturally in both the religious and secular realms.

The beginning of the Golden Age found Spain under Muslim rule, which continued in various regions conquered by the Christians. The leaders of the Jewish community and many of its members occupied prominent places in the ruling classes and were partners in determining the policies of the country. One cannot describe the economy of the country without mentioning the Jews who were the architects of the country's economic policies. But the Jews of that era were not only involved in international and national commerce. They were also the backbone of the crafts and industry of those times, just as they were the leaders in the various branches of agriculture. They contributed to the development of water management and irrigation methods, in introducing new crop species into Spain, in soil fertilization, in introducing crop rotation, and so on. Some scholars believe that the Arab Muslims, who had conquered Spain, were responsible for these developments. However, in our view, this was brought about by the Jews even though it occurred under the Arab conquest.

The Jews had significant independence in the field of Jewish culture. Their communities enjoyed almost total autonomy. The administration of the social life of the Jews was almost entirely in the hands of the Jewish authorities. The adjudication of disputes and the imposition of punishment were entrusted to the official Jewish institutions. Jewish courts of law were given coercive authority, even the right to impose major penalties including the death penalty, and this authority made the Jewish communities autonomous in every sense.

Extensive and new studies have summarized hundreds of years of the lives and activities of the Jewish communities in both Muslim and

Christian Spain and offer the inquiring student a fascinating realm of study.[1]

From the thirteenth to the fifteenth centuries, up to the expulsion of the Jews from Spain in 1492, there was a steady decline in the status which the Jewish communities had achieved in Spain, both in the few territories still controlled by the Muslims and, of course, in the majority of the territory, which had returned to Christian control. But there was relief even in those gloomy times, and on occasion it seemed that the Jewish communities had begun to flourish once again and their leaders occupied very important positions in the governing bodies. Several kings knew the strength of the Jew and his importance in vital areas of the government, particularly in policy-making and economics. Thus Jewish ministers occupied important positions in various royal courts.

One should note that the use of the Jewish mind in the courts of various Spanish kings stemmed not only from an appreciation of Jewish abilities but also from the fact that a high-ranking Jewish minister posed no threat to the king. While Jews could serve, they could never dream of becoming the head of state if the king should be overthrown. He would always remain an assistant, an advisor, a deputy, and that, too enhanced his status. One must say in defense of some of the kings of Spain that it was not easy for them to appoint a Jew or to favor the Jewish community, because to do so meant that the king would have to take on the Catholic hierarchy.

The Church regarded the Jewish people as a major opponent not only in the theological realm but also in the economic realm. The Christian monasteries and colleges taught people to read and write, and the Church hoped that all these people, not only the outstanding ones, would occupy places in the government. However, the Jews had gained entry to these areas. In many cities, the Jewish quarter, the Juderia, was moved from its original place to one which was under the protection of the king's palace. The old Jewish quarter, the Juderia Vieja of the tenth to the thirteenth centuries, had in most cases been built a considerable distance from the palaces and the prayer venues – both the mosques and the cathedrals – of the rulers. During the troubles of the thirteenth to the fifteenth centuries, most of these quarters had been vacated and the Jews had moved close to the palaces and to the homes of the governors. The new areas were known as the new Jewish quarter, the Juderia Nueva. This was the case in Segovia, Cordoba, Seville and in many other cities, including smaller ones.[2] The Jewish community's close proximity to the palace and to the army that protected it served as a defensive shield against the pogroms of the masses, which were carried out under the protection and encouragement of the Church.

During the peak of the Golden Age and in the centuries after it, until the expulsion of the Jews at the end of the fifteenth century,

Jewish communities were scattered throughout the length and breadth of Spain. There was almost no town or village of any consequence that did not have a Jewish settlement together with its essential communal buildings – a synagogue, a study hall, a *mikveh* (ritual bath), and a cemetery. Mention of these may be found in the Spanish archives, the literature, the Jewish documents, and archaeological and architectural discoveries. All of these enable us to plot a map of Jewish settlement, which spread throughout the Iberian peninsula.[3] It is worth noting that in other towns and villages there may have been other Jewish communities of whose existence we are not even aware. Even without them, there were hundreds of communities throughout the Iberian peninsula.

However, the Jewish settlement in Spain did not begin with the Muslim conquest of the peninsula at the beginning of the eighth century C.E. It preceded that conquest by many centuries.

The tradition prevalent in medieval Jewish Spain was that Jews had arrived in the country during King Solomon's time. In order to support this claim, tombstones were forged that allegedly showed that Jewish officials had arrived in Spain and built settlements there. However, the forgery was obvious because the writing on these tombstones was in square Hebrew script rather than in the ancient Hebrew script used during the First Temple era.[4] The forgery was intended primarily to provide the Jews with a defense in their dispute with the Christians regarding their responsibility for the crucifixion of Jesus. They wanted to prove that when that event took place in Jerusalem, the Jews had already been living in Spain for centuries. We can definitely

A Hebrew seal which was found in Megiddo, carrying the seal of the king's official: "To Shema, servant of Jeroboam." This is written in an ancient Hebrew script. The square script was instituted by Ezra the Scribe a few hundred years later.

state that there were Phoenician settlements in southern and eastern Spain during the ninth and eighth centuries B.C.E. Remnants of that era were discovered in archaeological digs in various locations in settlements and in graves, and among the pottery shards found there were ones typical of the Phoenician utensils of the ninth and eighth centuries B.C.E.,[5] but that is a far cry from proving that there was an established Jewish settlement in the area at that time.

We are on more solid ground when we speak of Jewish communities on Spanish soil during the Roman era. Studies by various scholars have shown that Jews lived in Spain during the first centuries of the Common Era and even in the last two centuries before it, not as individuals but in communities.[6]

Hispania, as the Romans called Spain, had been a country desired by the Romans as early as the third century B.C.E. After their victory in the Second Phoenician War, the Romans conquered southern and eastern Spain in 206 B.C.E. and fulfilled their dream of ruling over one of the richest countries along the Mediterranean shores. The final conquest of the Iberian peninsula was carried out in the years 26–19 B.C.E. during the reign of the emperor Augustus, who divided the country into three provinces. Jewish immigrants from the Land of Israel and from the Diaspora moved there. This virgin, vast land mass, which had few inhabitants and in which the Romans made major investments in development, attracted adventurers and those who had been forced out of other areas because of great congestion in the Land of Israel. Except for the first century B.C.E., during which there was fierce fighting in the land, sometimes between rival Roman forces, the Spanish provinces were relatively quiet. The Jews were thus able to establish flourishing, tranquil and secure communities on the Iberian peninsula.

In the first centuries of the Common Era, the Christian faith gradually percolated into the hearts of those living on the peninsula. Although there was something attractive about this newly arrived religion, the very act of accepting it indicated a certain protest against Roman rule. The first Christian Consilium, whose decisions have come down to us, took place in Spain in the city of Elvira, close to present-day Granada. It would appear that that was close to 306 C.E. Already at that conference, decisions were made that were intended to limit the Jews and to harm them. Among others, Christians were forbidden to inquire of Jews regarding the yield of their fields, could not take Jewish concubines, could not marry Jews, and could not dine with Jews.[7] This might have been in retaliation for similar decrees promulgated by the Jews against the Christian communities.

Minor changes in the relationship between the Christians and the Jews took place following the conquest by the Visigoths of Spain. In 415 C.E., the Visigoth battalions crossed the Pyrenees mountains and conquered the coastal strip, including the city of Barcelona. The conquest took more than fifty years, until the Visigoths finally managed to subdue most of the peninsula. They established their capital in Toledo, which later became the center of Jewish culture in Spain.

After establishing their rule in Spain, several of the kings enacted various laws and regulations which hampered the Jews, though not overly so. It is understandable that the Jewish-Christian confrontation in the Land of Israel and in the eastern communities and that brought about the enactment of draconian laws against the Jews there also affected the Visigoth rulers, but the Jews felt no substantial change and continued to live as they had in their communities, and maintained their heritage and activities.

One can see that the turning point came when the Visigoth kings decided to accept Catholicism and to prefer it over the Aryan Christian belief which they had accepted ever since they had adopted Christianity. It was King Reccared I who effected the religious revolution in 587 C.E. when he adopted Catholicism, along with many ministers and members of the royalty. The reason for this change was political rather than owing to any religious conviction. The king believed that it would be easier to rule Spain and to bring about its total unification if there was religious unity, specifically Catholic. Once he had converted, he became much more enthusiastic about his new religion, and that brought him to reconsider the Jews in his realm. Already then, the Catholic Church saw the solution to the Jewish problem as lying in the conversion of the Jews, even if this was carried out by force.[8] Laws and regulations which had been unheard of until that time in the west in general and in Spain in particular were now promulgated. The campaign in pursuit of the Jews was now underway and ultimately brought about the first destruction of the Jews in the Iberian peninsula.

From the material available to the historians, there is very little on the relationship between Reccared and the Jews. Afterwards, although not directly after him, came Sisebur, who ruled from 612 to 621. Sisebur was a very pious Catholic. He added to the laws enacted by Reccared and as a result was praised highly by the leaders of the Church, who regarded him as a faithful partner in their effort to destroy Judaism.

Sisebur was in very close contact with Bishop Isidore of Seville, and the latter even dedicated his book to him. The dedication, "Isidore to Sisebur, Master and Son,"[9] expresses briefly and decisively the new relationships which had developed between the Church and the monarchy. However, Sisebur did not content himself with merely updating the old laws and ensuring their enforcement, but also commanded that all Jews be baptized. Salo Baron has noted this sharp change in the life of the Jews of Spain, and in telling language he defined this action:

> Thus an era of a hundred years began of Sanctification of God's Name, which in some ways was a prelude to the tragedy eight hundred years later of the Jewry of Spain (1491–1492). As then (and in many other cases), here too the mass conversion did not bring about the immediate absorption of the converts within the majority of the population, but created a new group of converted Jews with clearly discernible characteristics. These converts, who by having taken this action of cutting themselves off from the Jewish People, had thereby annulled all the decrees which had been imposed on them as Jews, but neither the Christians nor the converted Jews themselves considered them to be full Christians. Up to the very last day of the rule of the Visigoths, these rules continued to regard, in almost the same breath, the Jews and those Jews who had been converted as being identical. In actuality, the term, without any adjectival limitation, referred in many cases to the convert himself, whereas in other cases the intention of the legislation, either knowingly or unknowingly, remained vague. The very existence of two types of Jews in the peninsula made it relatively easy for those who had been forced to convert to return to their own religion and fueled unceasing questions about their loyalty to their new religion.[10]

According to Rabilo,[11] these terrible decrees brought about the flight of Jews, some to southern France and others to North Africa, but most chose to convert and to secretly maintain their Judaism as *conversos.* According to him, some even managed to remain Jews and avoid baptism. The background for the formulation of Rabilo's views stems from what is known about the history of the Jews in Spain in later years – those illustrious communities which brought about the Golden Age. However, it appears that the act of conversion was much more significant and meaningful at that time, and in those years Spain became almost devoid of Jews. The large communities with which we will deal below have a different history, and their existence is linked to the Arab conquest and what followed it.

Nevertheless, it appears that the renewed limited settlement of Jews in Spain took place several years after the death of Sisebur. Suinthila, who reigned from 621 to 631 and who became king a few months after Sisebur's son, Reccared II, was the one behind the new developments. We do not have much information about Suinthila's reign, and the little that we have is cryptic. At the same time, some believe that during that time, Jews were not only invited back to Spain and permitted to maintain an independent lifestyle there, but the synagogues that had been seized and converted into churches were returned to them.[12] In any event, after a ten-year break in hostilities against the Jews during the reign of Suinthila, kings arose who were

The Catholic monarchs Ferdinand and Isabella, who expelled the Jews from Spain. An illustration in a manuscript of the 16th century. This is to be found in the University of Valladolid.

known for their cruel treatment of the Jews, and some even restored the decrees of Reccared I and implemented them in full. There were even such kings as Chintila (636–640) who ruled that no one but a Catholic was permitted to live in Spain, and members of all other religions must either convert or leave the country.[13] One cannot conclude from this decree that there were large Jewish communities in Spain, and it would appear that this directive was aimed primarily at Aryan Christians. Nevertheless, it appears that during the time of the Visigoth kings who followed Chintila there were periodic acts against the Jews. This was expressed both in the renewal of the old decrees and in the addition of new decrees that were worse than the earlier ones. From this we can deduce that there were Jewish communities in Spain in spite of the difficulties and the laws, and that before the adoption of Catholicism in the peninsula these communities were very strong, both in terms of numbers and in their loyalty to Judaism. Thus, attempts to convert them did not go easily.

Even during the reigns of the last Visigoth kings that preceded the Muslim conquest, various laws and decrees aimed at the Jews were a constant theme in the history of Spain of the seventh and early eighth centuries.

We can note several things in this regard: first, the Jews were very strong adherents of their faith. Their desire to observe and preserve Judaism was very powerful even when all types of economic decrees were directed against them and even at risk of their lives. However, since there were always Jews and Jewish communities in Spain, one may conclude that the enforcement of these laws was not always thorough.

One might regard this as an indication of the power of Jewish money and taxes to annul or at least moderate the kings' demands and decrees. The heavy pressure that Church leaders applied to the rulers to destroy Judaism were the basis for this anti-Jewish legislation, and there were two reasons for this: a) the Jews, thanks to their talents and education, had accumulated money and economic power. Now, whoever accumulated influence and economic advantages thereby weakened the absolute control of the Church over its subjects, most of whom were farmers and illiterates. Indeed, it was this economic power that was the basis of the control by the Church. (b) Moreover, it was very difficult for the Church to contend with the Jews as an existing entity, given the fact that according to it, Christianity was the embodiment of God's wishes. The existence of wealthy and flourishing Jewish communities did not match that assumption. If Jewish communities existed, they did so only in order to show the degradation of those who did not follow the True Faith. One could summarize its world view simply as the Church emerging victorious over the humiliated Synagogue.

As noted, a vibrant and thriving Judaism was not in keeping with this hypothesis. But the kings were aware of the economic asset that the Jewish community represented on the one hand, and the fact that no matter how lofty a rank a Jew might attain, he could never contend for the highest rank. Considerations such as these led to a situation in which the kings were torn between two conflicting paths: to act against the Jews and Judaism, but at the same time to make sure that the Jews were available when they were needed. Thus some kings imposed severe decrees but never really attempted to enforce them. Of course, there were exceptions to this rule: several kings whose relationship with the Church was weak, as well a few rare exceptions who were deeply devout and whose devotion affected their conduct.

A number of scholars support the view that the basis for the laws and decrees was primarily anti-Jewish sentiment[14] – i.e., pure anti-Semitism. According to others, though – and I include myself in this group – one must investigate carefully the economic background and the competitive factors that brought about conflicts between the Jews and the Church. The latter raised the flag of religion as a suitable and easy cover for destroying Judaism, thereby destroying the Jewish competition.[15]

This is not the place to expand on this issue beyond the needs of our study. The historical review is important to us only as it affects the synagogues in Spain. Rabilo summarized the topic as follows: "Before us we find that there were three distinct groups of Jews: Jews who refused to convert, Jews who were forcibly baptized against their will and who continued to practice their Judaism secretly, and Jews who were forcibly baptized but in the end accepted Christianity as their faith."[16] It is obvious that the synagogues could only be used by the first group – those who had refused to be converted – and even then it is logical to assume that the Jews worshipped in private homes rather than in their synagogues. By their very nature, public facilities could be attacked by anyone who so desired because the government did not provide any protection to the synagogues. One is able to learn about the existence of synagogues at that difficult time from the decrees which "forbade the building of new synagogues."[17]

This would imply that old synagogues still existed, except that during the reign of those kings who decreed that all foreigners must leave Spain or convert to Christianity, these buildings were evidently destroyed. If any still stood, they were transferred to Christian ownership. One can learn of the existence of synagogues both from the decrees that were made regarding them and from fragments of writings that mention their existence. Thus, for example, a tombstone inscribed both in Latin and Greek, reads: "In the name of God, Rabbi Lasis, son of the teacher (?), resting in peace, has found rest in this grave. Rabbi Latius, may he be blessed, has found rest here, of the archesynagogos of Kizikos. A righteous man… [may he be saved] from Gehinnom… may he rest upon his bier…."[18]

In this inscription, a person is listed as the "archesynagogos," i.e., the head of the synagogue. One should note that it is impossible to know from this inscription whether that term was prevalent in Spain or a title that Kizikos received in Asia Minor before moving to the Iberian peninsula. There are other fragmentary inscriptions which hint at the existence of synagogues, but all of these precede the Visigoth

A seven-branched candlestick which served as a symbol of the Jewish people and as a common decoration in ancient synagogues in the Land of Israel but which disappeared in the decorations of synagogues in the diaspora.

era, which established Catholicism as the only Christian doctrine in Spain.[19] We can summarize and state that there were many magnificent synagogues in Spain even before the Arab conquest.

In the hundred years before the Arab invasion of Spain, almost all of Spanish Jewry was destroyed because of mass conversions and expulsions from the Iberian peninsula. When the Arab conquest –which was liberal toward the Jews – took place, the few who had remained, along with the forced converts to Christianity who still carried their ancestors' faith in their hearts, were able to live once more as proud Jews. However, these were not the builders of the great Spanish Jewry from the tenth century on. They merely joined many others who had just come to Spain and together established the Golden Age, whose role in the life of our people was essential to the existence of our nation and its continuity.

The greatest scholars of Jewish history in the Middle Ages all spoke of the existence of the glorious Jewish existence in Spain before the Arab conquest. They were also very well aware of the difficult years suffered by the Jews and Judaism in the last hundred years of Visigoth rule and the destruction they suffered at that time. However, when they sought the source for the origins of the Jews of the Golden Age, they hit a blank wall. Whence did the Jewish people in its newly glorious era spring on Spanish soil? They therefore assumed that the forced conversions were not as serious as they appear in the sources and studies. Now, no one can deny that the Jewish People again in their hearts flourished once more in Spain.[20] However, we are faced with a dearth of sources and an absence of studies. It is understandable that while this hypothesis can be maintained, another hypothesis can also be entertained, which appears to me to be preferable, and its main thesis is that the rejuvenation was brought about by the waves of new Jewish immigrants who came to Spain following the Arab-Islamic conquest.

In the year 681 C.E., Arab troops appeared off the coast of Spain. All of north Africa had been conquered, and the area of the Magreb (modern-day Morocco) was subject to the Muslim yoke. It took thirty years for the Muslim cavalry to cross the Mediterranean at the place where it meets up with the Atlantic Ocean, and they penetrated into the Iberian peninsula. The renowned Arab general, Táriq-ibn-Ziyád, commanded the glorious military campaign. He moved his troops at night and concentrated them in the massive caves on the mountain cliffs, an area which had been constructed by the Romans, who had named it Julia Calpe. At the time it was a ghost town and was uninhabited. The Visigoth kings were not sufficiently alert to the appetite of the Muslims and their actions. Ever since that time, the mountain cliff has been named after Mount Tariq, or in Arabic "Jebel Tariq," or as it is known today, "Gibraltar." At the end of April of the year 711, Spain entered a new historical era. In Jewish annals, this date can be regarded as the beginning of a new era for the Jews of the west, an era which made a major impact on the history of the Jewish People throughout the world. The greatest time of the Golden Age of the Jews of Spain had begun, with the Jewish People at its best.[21] In a short time, the entire peninsula was captured by the Muslims, except for a few isolated parts in the northwest. The Arabs even crossed the Pyrenees and entered France, but they were repulsed and the border between Christian Europe and the mighty Muslim empire was set along the Pyrenees mountains. This was only a few decades after the new religion, the one preached by Muhammad, had broken out of the Arabian peninsula and flooded the Middle East and northern Africa.

The Arab conquest was unlike many of the conquests in the Middle East. The Arabs understood that if they wanted to hold onto the numerous tracts of land which they had conquered, they had to build on the fears of those who had been conquered and the first brilliant successes of the conquerors, and to bring the majority of the inhabitants of their conquered territories under the fold of the new religion, Islam. Drastic Islamic measures were taken in the area, with the slogan, "The religion of Islam through the sword." What it meant was that either the person converted or was to be put to death. Many people were unable to withstand these decrees, and many countries conquered by the Muslims became Muslim. Those who showed stubborn resistance were the Zoroastrian Persians, the Christians, and many Jews. The Muslim conquerors realized that if they continued with their strong pressure on these groups, they had more to lose than to gain: they would gain territory, but there would no one to work the land there. They also understood that building the public administration of the new empire would require the cooperation of the educated people among those who had been conquered, and that destroying them would mean destroying the entire empire. That was why the draconian law that insisted that anyone who did not convert would be put to death was not applied to these groups. Instead, they were left alive and became known as "the People of the Book," i.e., those who accepted the holy works which Islam recognized as holy. They were given protection under the designation *dhimmi* and were permitted to maintain their own religions and not to convert.

In return for this privilege, they had to pay heavy taxes on their earnings in agriculture. In other words, they received religious freedom in return for heavy taxation. This especially affected the Jews in the Land of Israel and in Babylon, whose primary occupation was farming. As a result, many communities in the Land of Israel were almost wiped out. Anyone who converted to Islam was exempt from these taxes, while those who refused to do so were forced to pay them. It was impossible to live as a farmer under these conditions.

Many settlements and heretofore successful agricultural tracts had to be abandoned. However, there is nothing bad without some good. The Arab conquest brought about a migration to the cities and new occupational opportunities for the Jews.

After things had calmed down in the world and the Arab conquest had stabilized and achieved the silent approval of Christian Europe, international trade had to return to what it had been earlier. The world could not survive without that trade.

International trade became a fruitful avenue for the Jews where they could be extremely successful. Even though neither the Christians nor the Muslims particularly admired them, each group hated the other much more. The Jews were thus able to enter this vacuum and to serve as brokers in international trade. One should add to this their international communication skills because of their common language; their education, which enabled them to understand the intricacies of international trade; and most of all, Jewish law, which served as a type of legal system in a world in which there was no international trade law. These and other factors can explain why trade became an excellent refuge for the Jews and a place to turn after they had been evicted from their farms, this being especially true in the Land of Israel. The eighth century was the one during which the Jews in the Land of Israel abandoned agriculture. The place where they took refuge, which was a trade center, was Spain – in the Ummayad Caliphate whose capital was Cordoba, following the overthrow of the Abbasid Caliphate. The new Caliphate, which had just been established (in 750 C.E.), needed all types of administrators, and here too the Jews could offer excellent services. Thus we have a situation where Jews left the east, the Land of Israel, and were absorbed in the west, especially in Spain. It was this nucleus that later formed the Golden Age of Spain. The culture of the Golden Age was a continuation of the culture of the Land of Israel. The names of the people and the creative spirit were that of the Land of Israel. This was not a continuation of Spanish Jewry of the time before the Catholic Visigoth kings, but rather the embodiment of the world of the Land of Israel.[22] One needs to tie this to the architecture of the synagogue, which carried and was permeated with the flavor of the Land of Israel, obviously under the influence of the architecture of Spain of those days and the limitations of building under foreign rule.

Although the era of the Ummayad Caliphate lasted long, from its very beginning the Christians in the north began to organize, amass an army and prepare to retake the country. The Reconquista movement, namely the movement to free the land from the Muslims, was born. It took seven hundred years for this process to be completed, culminating in the conquest of Granada in 1492, the same year in which the Jews were expelled from Spain. This is not the place to review these events or to review Jewish life against the background of these events. All of these have been the subjects of excellent studies, especially those of Baer and Ashtori.[23]

However, the events in which the Muslims and Christians were involved were not the only ones to affect the Jews. There were wars and peace treaties between the different Christian principalities in the north, and regime changes within the areas still under Muslim rule in the north. Invasions from North Africa brought about the destruction of dynasties and their replacement by other ones. The character of the rulers and the constraints on them had a direct bearing on the way they treated the Jews. We would like to stress here what we know – specifically, that there were terrible times for the Jews under certain Muslim rulers and glorious days of creativity and of the development of their culture under Christian kings in the north. There were Catholic kings under whom Judaism flourished until the end of the fourteenth century. That time period marked a turning point in the relationship between the monarchy and the Jews as a result of increasing pressure by the Church, which was strengthening its position throughout Spain.

The remnants of the architecture of synagogues that are found in Spain in our day are all from the era of Christian rule in Spain of the twelfth and thirteenth centuries. No traces have been found of synagogues in the areas controlled by the Muslims, just as there are no remains of synagogues that existed in the era before the Muslim conquest, in spite of our historical knowledge of their existence.

Toledo, the Shmuel HaLevi Synagogue, a reconstructed perspective of the synagogue structure. The view is from the southwest.

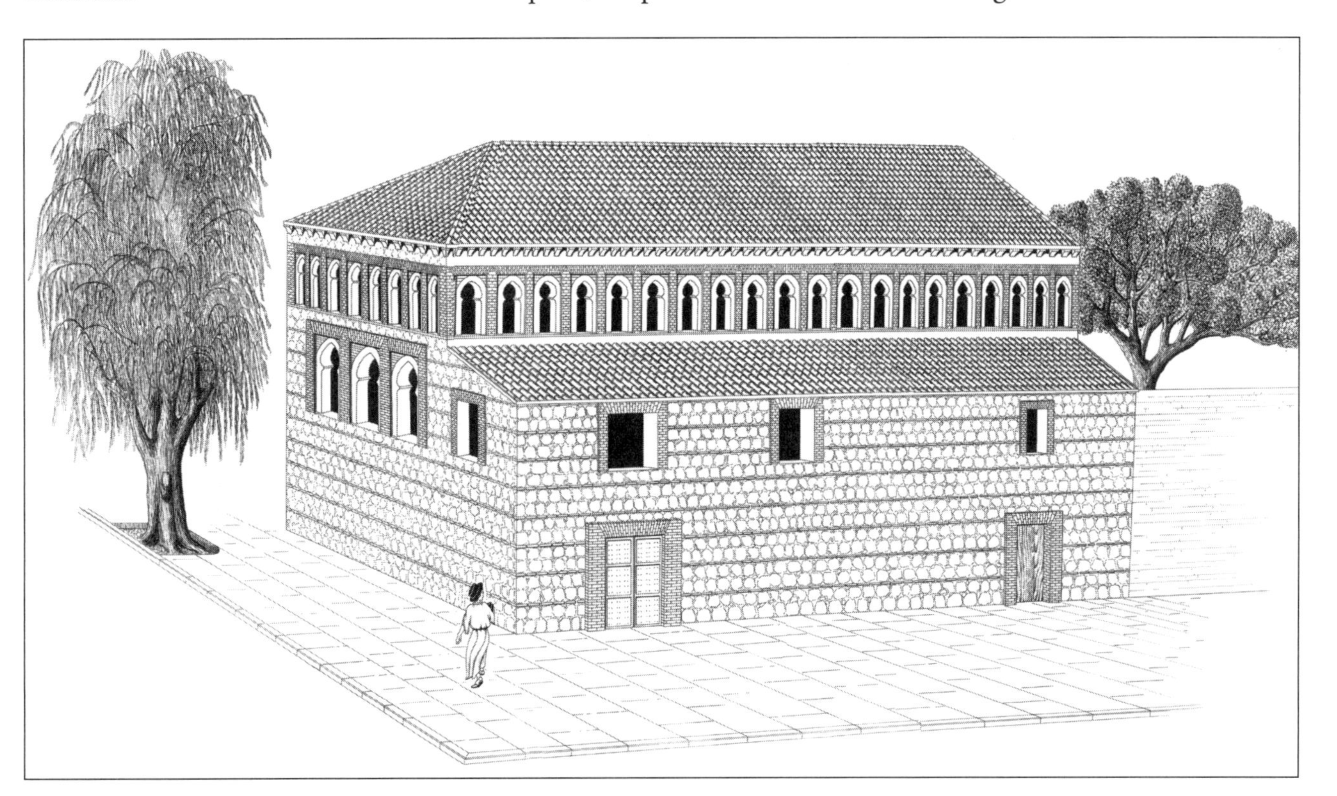

Chapter 2 Synagogues in Spain According to the Sources and Research

Throughout all generations and in every place where Jews have lived, the most clearly visible and unmistakably public Jewish institution has been the synagogue. Alongside the synagogue and under its aegis and administration, other public institutions were constructed including the study hall, yeshivah, and *mikveh* (plural: *mikva'ot*). This group of buildings was the essential communal center, without which committed Jews could not live. An examination of the documents of those times yields dozens of sources and information that shed light on the way the synagogues and other institutions functioned. The written material we have paints a picture for us of hundreds of synagogues that functioned both in Spain under the Muslim-Arab conquest and in the countries and principalities under Christian rule throughout the Iberian peninsula. In the eleventh and twelfth centuries, the Mozarabs, a fanatic Muslim sect whose origins were in north Africa, ruled in southern Spain. During their reign, in Cordoba alone forty synagogues were destroyed.[1]

Several decades later, most of the territory in the south was conquered by the Christian kings of Spain. In 1378, more than a hundred years after Seville had been conquered and had become Christian territory, the city was visited by Archdeacon Ferdinand Martinez, who preached publicly there. In his speeches, he demanded that the Jewish quarter in Seville be closed and that the twenty-three synagogues in it be destroyed.[2]

From this we can understand the remarkable power of the Jews in Spain at that time. A similar number of synagogues, or sometimes a somewhat smaller number, was to be found in the other Spanish cities: Toledo, Barcelona, Gerona, Granada, Malaga, Cordoba, and others. A special case was the city of Lucena, about 130 km. (78 miles) eastern of Seville and about 100 km. (60 miles) north of Malaga. This city, in the middle of agricultural land in southern Spain, was populated only by Jews, including some who earned their living from farming or from crafts. One may assume that there were a number of synagogues in this city.[3] The Jewish population in Spain from the tenth to the fourteenth centuries lived in dozens of settlements, including in small agricultural villages and large cities, where large communities resided. This implies that there were hundreds of synagogues in the Iberian peninsula.

The synagogue was not only a place for prayer but also served as the focus for daily life. If a child was circumcised, the elaborate ceremony took place in the synagogue. Naturally, marriages were also solemnized there, and it was the place where the seven days of mourning for a dead relative were concluded. At the end of the seven days of mourning, the first thing the mourners did was to go to the synagogue to pray.[4] One should note that after the seven days of mourning the mourners did not return to their customary seat in the synagogue, but sat in a different place. Only some time later did they return to their own seats.

The community leaders tried to purchase land around the synagogue both for their communal institutions and for a garden. Sometimes they were unsuccessful and the *mikveh* had to be built separately. One of the important *mikva'ot* in Toledo is about thirty meters (more than thirty yards) from the Santa Maria la Blanca (the White Saint Mary) synagogue.[5] We should be more accurate and note that due to the changes that took place in the neighborhood of the synagogue in the last seven hundred years, we cannot tell whether at the time the *mikveh* and the synagogue were not all part of a single synagogue complex, and it is possible that a new rezoning of this area in Toledo, after the expulsion of the Jews in 1492, caused this apparent distance between the two.

The planting of gardens around synagogues was done under the influence of Muslim architects. In these gardens there were water wells that fed basins and troughs meant for purifying oneself before one entered the synagogue, as is the practice among Muslims.[6] The garden around the synagogue also had another purpose, as it was there that a *sukkah* was built for the *Sukkot* festival. Because of the crowded conditions of housing in those days and because of the small size of the dwellings, very few people had the ability to build a private *sukkah* for their own family. In order to enable the community to participate in this *mitzvah*, a public *sukkah* was built in the synagogue courtyard, and that was where everyone went to eat during the festival.[7] This arrangement was due to circumstances in the Diaspora, even though the religious heads of the Jewish community in the Land of Israel and in Babylon, the Geonim, were not in favor of this. In the rabbis' responsa, we can see that according to them, unless one actually built a *sukkah* for himself and his family, he has not fulfilled the requirements of the *mitzvah*. At the same time, though, the rabbis required the building of a *sukkah* in each synagogue courtyard for visitors to the city and for tradesmen and wayfarers, so that they, too, could fulfill the *mitzvah*.

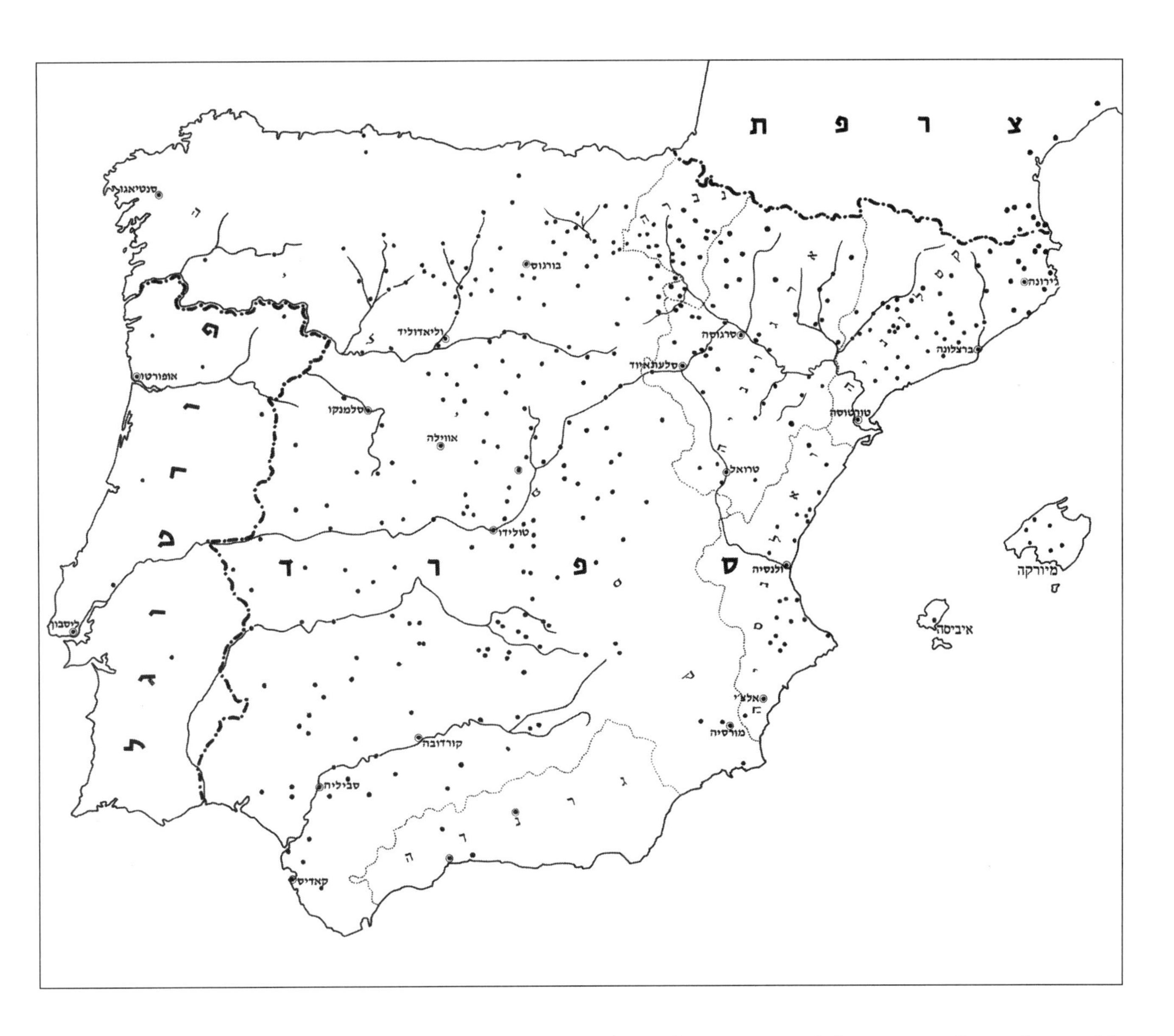

Spain, the population density of Jews in the Spanish cities and periphery, according to Ber.

The large number of synagogues did not stem from the wealth of the communities and their desire to be ostentatious or to glorify their community heads. This was a consequence of living under a foreign regime that was hostile to Jews on the one hand, and from the organizational and internal-social structure of the community on the other. Because of the mean-spiritedness of the Christian regimes and their adherents and because of the Church's hostility to the very existence of the Jews, the Jews were not permitted to build beautiful or large structures. They were thus forced to build synagogues that were considerably smaller than the Christian churches, and this disparity was all the more pronounced when we compare the synagogues to cathedrals. Thus the average non-Jewish citizen would be able to sense the degradation of Judaism when compared to Christianity. As there were a large number of Jews in each city, where one synagogue could not possibly be enough, the Jews were forced to build several small synagogues to enable all those who needed these services to receive them through this structure and its institutions. One should stress, though, that in spite of what we have just stated, we do have evidence of large synagogues, which were referred to as "Sinagoga Mayor." One may thus assume that among the hundreds of synagogues, a number were large, especially in the cities. These large synagogues had a higher status that the others. Sometimes, the street on which a large synagogue stood was called "the Street of the Large Synagogue" (Calle de la Sinagoga Mayor). That, for example, was the case in the Jewish Quarter of Barcelona in the first centuries after the first millennium C.E.[8] In other cities, too, there is mention of large synagogues alongside smaller ones, as in Toledo.[9] However, even these synagogues, which were given such grand names, were in no way as large as the large churches and even smaller when compared to cathedrals.

Since many synagogues were built in the different neighborhoods of the Jewish communities, each synagogue had its own individual character. Various groups of tradesmen in certain realms preferred to pray together, and therefore they established their own synagogues. Thus, for example, there were synagogues for shoemakers, for weavers, for tailors, and for the other crafts.[10] This division was not only by the different occupations, but also based on socio-economic status or based on family origins. Sometimes, a wealthy family could afford to build a synagogue for its family members and friends. In Toledo, for example, there was a synagogue for people who had lived in Cordoba and who had left that city because of the pressure of the hostile Muslim regime and had moved to Christian Toledo, which at that time was friendly toward the Jews. It was known as the "Cartabi (i.e., Cordoba) Synagogue." In Toledo there was also a synagogue named after the Ben Abidraham family,[11] evidently a family that was involved in banking and finance. Other synagogues there were the Solokaya (?) Synagogue and the Ben Aryeh Synagogue. The literature also mentions buildings near synagogues which were known by the names of those who taught there or who donated funds for their construction. In Toledo, for example, there was the *Midrash Ben Anku'a*, (?) which was a corruption of the name of the well-known Elnekaveh family, or the *Midrash Ben Ye'aker*, the *Midrash R. Yisrael*, and others.[12]

The various religious functionaries in the synagogues and other institutions were recognized by the government and even enjoyed tax reductions. Up to the end of the fourteenth century, the Christian kings in Spain even ensured the rights of the various communities to their synagogues and communal institutions.[13] In several places the kings regarded the synagogues as the place to turn to when the royal messengers needed to gather the Jewish community together. It was there, for example, that great disputations run by the Dominican monks on behalf of the Crown and the Church were held between Christians and Jews.[14] The most famous debate was conducted in the synagogue in Barcelona with Nahmanides as the disputant for the Jewish side, and in addition to the Dominican monks and their heads, the king of Catalonia, James I, was present. On that Sabbath, the king himself preached in the synagogue, a very unusual action, unheard of in the entire history of the Middle Ages.[15] Thus, even though the Jews were persecuted, their synagogues remained standing since the government used them for its own purposes. Even though the monarchy was engaged in a struggle with Judaism, for its own reasons it left the synagogues in the Jews' hands and even assisted in their maintenance. For their part, the Jews went out of their way to construct more and more synagogues and to beautify them, knowing that this was almost the only possible and practical way to preserve their Judaism in so hostile, vindictive, and malicious an environment as Christian Spain. Even in the fifteenth century, when the Church and the royal court increased the pressure on the Jews, the kings nevertheless promulgated decrees about constructing and maintaining synagogues.

Don Abraham Benveniste was made the Rabbi of the Court of King Juan II, and his official title was "Rab de la Corte." His position made him responsible for all the Jewish communities in Castile, the supreme judge of the Jewish public, and the one who appointed *parnasim* (lay leaders) and judges to administer Jewish affairs. He also had the authority to distribute the taxes of all the Jewish communities. In 1432 he assembled all the leaders of the Jewish communities and scholars and presented to them the book of regulations that he had written. As far as the topic at hand here is concerned, the regulation regarding the synagogues is important, for it states there that "any community having ten families or more shall establish a place for prayers.... A fine shall be imposed on anyone who fails to come to public prayers in the morning or evening unless he is prevented by some valid reason."[16]

The text indicates to us a Jewish world rich in synagogue buildings. The question thus to be asked is: What has remained physically of all these buildings?

The sources mention the hard times which the synagogues in Spain were subject to. The forced conversions and the persecution of Jews, which was the lot of the Jewish communities until the Arabic conquest, certainly affected the communal synagogues adversely. Some were destroyed, others torn down, others burned, while others were seized by the Christian authorities for their own needs. These were converted into churches. Of all of the physical evidence of that time which has been discovered, but a single solitary remnant of one synagogue has been found. This was a synagogue in Elche, in eastern Spain, north of Alicante. From the ruins we can see that it had a simple basic structure with a mosaic floor, and that there was a semicircular niche on the eastern wall. Indeed, the first ones to publish this find believed that it had been a church. Today, though, the more prevalent view is that it was the synagogue of the Elche community which was later converted into a church. Is plan was similar to the synagogues of the Byzantine era in the Land of Israel.[17] However, before we discuss actual ruins, let us go back to the sources.

Throughout the time the Jews lived in Spain, both under Muslim and under Christian rule, we find that the Jewish communities were sometimes raised to the heights and at other times dashed to the ground, from positions almost at the very top of the pyramid to the very depths, and this situation was cyclical until the expulsion in 1492. Each wave of decrees brought about the destruction of some synagogues and the transformation of others into churches. This is not the place to discuss more substantial issues such as forced conversions, Jews surrendering their lives for their beliefs, and various major attacks that were aimed at both body and soul, as our study deals with buildings. We will therefore focus on the structure of the synagogues.

A very significant event in this regard was the ascent of Ferrard Martinez to the position of archbishop of Seville. His anti-Jewish speeches soon began to bear fruit. Already in 1390 the church deacons received specific orders to destroy all the synagogues in the district. The anti-Jewish turmoil that began reached its peak in 1391 and continued until 1415, and is known in the annals of Spanish Jewry as the pogrom of the Hebrew year 5151. The wave of bloodshed began in the south and spread throughout Castile, bursting out in the north like an avalanche. In those years, entire Jewish communities were wiped out, the children either killed or forcibly converted. Most of the synagogues were destroyed, while many others were seized

The Cathedral of Saragossa, "Our Lady of the Pillar," on the banks of the Ebro river; the Jewish Quarter of the city was to its west.

by the Christian authorities and made into churches. That was the case in Seville, Cordoba, Toledo, and every other place throughout Spain.[18]

During those terrible years there were also attempts to prevent these events from taking place. In the kingdom of Aragon, for example, the king forbade the Church from converting those Jews who had found refuge with their Christian friends. He also forbade the conversion of synagogues into churches. Although he wanted to bring things back to the state that had preceded the pogroms, he never managed to do anything about it, although in some areas there was relative calm.[19]

All the actions aimed by the palace of King Juan I in his capital, Zaragoza, and that were meant to calm things down to the state that had existed before the disturbances failed. In Barcelona, for example, the king set aside an area for a new synagogue and wanted to return the old cemetery to Jewish hands, but his plan never went beyond the drawing boards. Furthermore, in 1401 King Martin totally forbade the reconstruction of a Jewish community in Barcelona after the pogroms that had driven the Jews from there. A hundred years before the expulsion from Spain, Barcelona and entire regions of Catalonia and Aragon were entirely empty of Jews. The Jewish quarters were seized by the urban Christian mobs and those synagogues that were not destroyed were made into churches.[20]

The following years were marked by ever more severe decrees and of the shedding of Jewish blood. This had a devastating effect on the synagogues, with widespread destruction and transformation into churches. A Dominican friar of Valencia named Vicente Ferrer spearheaded a religious campaign throughout Castile. With his extraordinary speaking ability he was able to draw close to those Jews who had been beaten and feared for their lives and to convert many of them. In several places he entered synagogues and consecrated them to the Catholic Church, so that they could be used for Christian ritual.[21]

These events were a clear indication of what would occur throughout the fifteenth century up to the expulsion, even though a ray of light illuminated the darkness now and then. However, the general picture in Spain throughout that time was one of waves of persecution, the destruction of Jewish property, and the conversion of synagogues, at best, into churches. In many places they did not even bother to convert the synagogues into churches, but made them the private property of those in charge of the cities and towns. The underlying motive of these actions was to desecrate the synagogues even if all the members of the community had been slaughtered, converted, or had left the area. This humiliation may have been necessary in order to dissuade converts from believing that a time might come when they could profess their Judaism openly once more. This was considered a war to the finish by

Christianity against Judaism, and it included the Christians taking out their wrath against the very wood and stone of the synagogues. There are accounts of synagogues that the local populace converted into barns. Others were turned into quarantine stations for people who had been bitten by rabid dogs, while still others became hospitals for the chronically ill, whom the people felt should be isolated. Hundreds of buildings were put to the torch, their ruins silent testimony to glorious communities that had been destroyed. Many centuries of unintentional or deliberate forgetfulness passed, and vital information about the Jewish construction vanished completely.

In the nineteenth century scholars and academics began to take an interest in the history of the Jews in Spain. Even though the great era of world tourism of the twentieth century had not yet begun, the Spanish, particularly after World War II, began to think of how to preserve the remnants of the various synagogues and to preserve them as national monuments22 and as memorials to the Jewish contribution to the history of Spain. Two synagogues in Toledo, the capital of Spanish Jewry under the Christian rule, which had been converted to churches, were cleared out and reconstructed according to their original design. These were the church known as El Transito, which had originally been a synagogue, and the Church of Santa Maria la Blanca, which had also been converted from a synagogue to a hospital and then to a church. One may note parenthetically that when synagogues or mosques were converted to churches, the appellation "the white" or "the light" was added to their name, such as Santa Maria la Blanca, while a mosque which had been converted to a church was named Cristo de la Luz, which means "Jesus, the Messiah of light." These names were meant to indicate that these buildings, which according to the Christians had been the dwelling places of Satan when they had been synagogues or mosques, were churches in which light now dwelled. Thus, they were now buildings meant for the greater glory of Jesus and of God. Throughout Spain one can find this phenomenon repeated time and again, for that same reason.[23]

Despite Franco's ties with the Nazis, under his rule Spanish scholars continued to study the history of the Jewish community in Spain, and important publications appeared during those years. Francisco Cantera-Burgos, one of the best scholars of the history of the Jews of Spain, published a volume about synagogues in Spain entitled *Sinagogas Españoles*[24] While this work does not go into any in-depth study of the architecture, an analysis of the inscriptions and historical background is of great value. Cantera-Burgos's contribution to the study of synagogues is of great importance. He and Millas, another fellow of the academy, published an important book about the Hebrew inscriptions in Spain, including those in the synagogues, entitled *Les Inscripciones Hebraicas de España*[25]

"Sefarad," the name of a quarterly which appears in Madrid. This quarterly publishes studies in the realm of Judaism, and especially in regard to Spanish Jewry and its past.

Several years ago, a popular guide to Jewish sites in Spain, including cities and synagogues, was published: *A Guide to Spanish Jewry* by Joan Atienza.[26] While it was written as a popular guide, it is of great importance since the accelerated development within Spain has resulted in the destruction of relics which could still be studied recently. Therefore, this guide took a snapshot of a situation that is disappearing before our eyes. At the end of the 1960s, a Jewish-American scholar named Don A. Halperin traveled to Spain in order to study the synagogues there, and after several months published a volume entitled *The Ancient Synagogues of the Iberian Peninsula*.[27] This study contains several innovations, the most important of which is the identification of several ruins of synagogues that had were previously unknown. Halperin deals both with the general historical background and a preliminary architectural analysis. This study which was conducted more than thirty-five years ago, documented several structures that no longer exist.

The present work, *Synagogues in Spain*[28] is the product of a study by an Israeli scholar who wished to contribute to research on Spanish Jewry. This is the first comprehensive Israeli study that deals with all aspects of the topic. The scholars who have studied ancient synagogues in the various lands of Jewish dispersion did not study the synagogues in Spain. Among the most important Israeli scholars of synagogues one must mention Pinkerfeld, who described these relics briefly in his books[29] but did not study these first-hand. Although he always said that at some future time he would like to return to dealing with the synagogues in Spain, his sudden murder by Arab Legion troops in 1956 destroyed that dream. Since other Israeli studies are generally based on quotes from foreign and Hebrew sources, they are not innovative. Furthermore, they often contain errors as copied from the original sources that they quote.[30]

What difficulties are encountered by one who wishes to write a study the synagogues of Spain? First and foremost, there are the objective difficulties stemming from the fact that at least five hundred years and sometimes as many as seven hundred years have elapsed since these buildings were first built. Their construction was simple, and they were not meant to stand for hundreds of years. It is understandable that they have been damaged considerably. One should note that an added difficulty was the alienation of the local Christian populace as far as these ruins were concerned, for they regarded them as abominable. This immediately makes it difficult for the scholar even to locate the synagogues in settlements throughout all of Spain. After such a site is located, it is clear that to study it require a great deal of resources, sometimes even in excavating and measuring in the middle of a residential area. This requires obtaining the requisite licenses, a large amount of money, and the assistance of the Church, which is in most cases the owner or has a claim to the property. All of these problems made it almost impossible for such a study to be pursued at the initiative of an individual. What this project needs is a foundation – Israeli or Jewish – that will invest resources and thought in research about the synagogues, one of the most fascinating and important subjects the history of the Jews of Spain.

One should also emphasize that the time to be able to conduct such a study is fast drawing to a close, for in the past years Spain is speedily joining the countries of western Europe. This has resulted in accelerated growth and construction, both in the infrastructure and in the roads, and this has often included the destruction of ancient buildings, including the ruins of synagogues, where such destruction eliminates any possibility of future research. It is therefore imperative that the proper steps be taken before it is too late.

Chapter 3 The Architecture of the Spanish Synagogues: A Brand Plucked from the Fire

But a Few of Hundreds

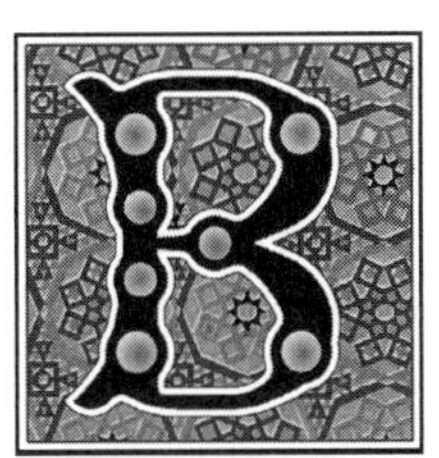

y the time of the Arab conquest of the Iberian peninsula in the eighth century C.E., the area contained dozens – if not hundreds – of synagogues. Ever since the Jewish population had settled in the area in the first centuries C.E. under the protection of the Roman Empire, the peninsula had been host to a large number of Jews and the many public buildings that served their needs. We have information regarding that era from documents of those days which dealt with the Jewish communities. Most of this information comes from the onerous decrees imposed on the Jews of Spain before the Arab conquest, when Spain was under the rule of the Visigoth kings, and especially in the sixth and seventh centuries C.E. During that time, when the Jews were persecuted, the synagogues also suffered, since they were Jewish communal centers. Some synagogues were burned, others demolished, and the majority were simply seized from their lawful owners and converted into churches. We are unable to estimate how many of the latter were restored to their rightful owners after the Arab conquest in the eighth century. Nor is it possible to ascertain clearly which of these buildings were restored, which could still be used, especially as communal buildings, and whether the Arab conquerors were willing to enter into confrontations with the local Christian population by returning synagogues that had been converted to churches to their lawful owners. The written documentation of the time is silent about this aspect. Nor do we have any archaeological or architectural ruins of the era which predates the Arab conquest. Of course this absence of information may simply be attributed to the fact that this topic, accompanied by the necessary archaeological digs, has not yet been explored in depth.

From the Arab conquest in the eighth century until the fifteenth century, Jewish communities in Spain flourished. We have written historical documentation regarding the existence of synagogues during that time. In this era the history of the Jews, their lives and deeds in Spain, are well documented, this being a unique case regarding the history of Jews throughout the world in those generations. The great amount of information available includes Spain under the rule of various groups of Muslim Arabs, as well as those areas that the Christians retook from the Muslims. It is a fact that the many Jewish communities had many synagogues. Of the hundreds of synagogues of that time we have very scant remains, and even these are only from the second half of that era, between the twelfth and fifteenth centuries. It is obvious that whatever remnants of these hundreds of synagogues that still exist are no longer used for their original purpose. Some were converted into churches, three were made into tourist sites that preserve a chapter in the history of Spain – specifically, the part played by the Jews in the construction of the glorious history of Spain. Yet the vast majority of them are still waiting to be studied properly because they are off the beaten track in small towns and villages, where they lie forsaken and ruined or have been put to use by individuals or communities for various purposes such as granaries and stables.

A study of the architecture of the synagogues in Spain must therefore be based on the minute fraction of those that still exist. Even from the few remaining ruins, one can deduce that there was no unified, overall plan regarding the synagogue structures. This is nothing unusual but is in keeping with what has been learned regarding other places and earlier eras, during those times and later ones. Unlike the churches, the synagogues did not have a unified plan, even though the ceremonial functions for which they were used were all identical. Many subjective factors were involved, such as the size of the area upon which the synagogue was constructed, the wealth of the community and the resources available to it, their view of the individual within society, and the status of women. All of these resulted in the formulation of architectural plans that differed from one building to another.

From the written documentation, it appears that the decorations in the synagogues, especially regarding their interiors, showed far-reaching changes in the second quarter of the second millennium – in the thirteenth century, very severe restrictions were imposed regarding the decoration of the synagogue interior.[1]

At that time, Jewish law instituted severe restrictions regarding paintings on the walls of the synagogue. Therefore, one cannot talk in one breath about the interior decoration of the synagogue in the first millennium C.E. and its decoration in the first half of the second millennium.

Of the hundreds of synagogues that served the Jews of Spain, today there are only five structures that were indubitably synagogues. There are also several buildings that are used as churches, and by all logic these, too, were once synagogues. So, too, are there neglected fragmentary remains of synagogues. This work will bring together all of this material

Examples of horseshoe arches in the Mudejar style, which was common in the architecture of the synagogues in Spain.

and discuss it. Jewish ritual required the existence of various objects and certain internal structures within the building, such as the *hekhal* (the "Holy Ark"), the *tevah* or *bimah*, seating arrangements for the notables and the other members of the congregation, a women's section, and so on. Some of these were made of wood, and understandably rotted over the years and left nothing behind. Those appurtenances built of tougher materials were removed by the Christians when the buildings were converted into churches or for other uses. In spite of that, when we discuss the architecture of the Spanish synagogues, we will discuss the internal structure of the synagogues based on drawings of those days and especially on miniatures that decorated various religious and secular books, especially Passover *Haggadot*. To this we will add theoretical discussions, and we will compare synagogues of later eras that preserved the tradition of the Spanish synagogues, such as those in Italy and in north Africa, and especially those synagogues that have been studied and investigated, such as those of Tunis.[2]

Those synagogues that are still intact, which have remained to this day in spite of the vicissitudes of time and history, and which thus serve as a basis for our discussion include: the New Synagogue in Toledo, known also as the Synagogue of Joseph ibn Shoshan, and which is now known as Sinagoga Santa Maria la Blanca.[3] At the time of the expulsion, this building was seized from the Jews but was not destroyed as those who had seized it turned it to their own uses. That was also the case with another synagogue in Toledo, the synagogue of Samuel ha-Levi Abulafia, which has now become a museum of the history of Spanish Jewry and is known as Sinagogo del Transito de Nuestra Señora – the Synagogue of the Transit of Our Lady. Both of these synagogues are in Toledo, the capital of ancient Castile. In addition to these, there is another synagogue in Castile, in Segovia, which had also been seized and converted into a church. Even though this church burned down at the beginning of the twentieth century, it was rebuilt according to its original specifications and thus enables us to learn from its structure. This synagogue is now known as Corpus Christi ("The Body of Christ").

The other two intact synagogues are in Andalusia, in southern Spain. They date from the thirteenth century, in other words in an era where southern Spain, with the exception of Granada, was already under Christian rule. One synagogue, which is located in Seville, in the center of the Jewish Quarter, was used by the residents of the market neighborhood. It, too, was seized and converted into a church and is still in use as a church to this day, known as Santa Maria la Blanca.

All four of these structures are large and are worthy of being called synagogues, but the fifth, which is located in the center of Cordoba's Jewish Quarter, is only a small prayer room, a side room of what was once a study hall or yeshivah. Another possibility is that it was a private prayer chapel in the home of a wealthy Jewish notable. Tradition has it that this was the synagogue of Maimon, the father of the illustrious Maimonides, and that this is the house in which Maimonides was born. However, the family was forced to flee to Morocco and from there to the Land of Israel and then to Egypt. Maimonides was born in the twelfth century, whereas the inscription in this prayer chapel states that it was built in the thirteenth. It is possible that the room was converted to a prayer chapel during the thirteenth century and that is what the inscription commemorates.

Alongside the five large synagogues we find other, more modest structures in Caceres, Avila, Tudela, and in several small villages, the ruins of which serve as the basis for the present study.[4]

The Synagogue, its Site, and its Status

ewish law from the time of the Mishnah states: "The residents of a town force one another to build a synagogue and to buy a Torah scroll, along with [scrolls of] the Prophets and the Hagiographa." This law shows to what extent a synagogue was important to the Jewish community even from the very outset. Later traditions added various demands and instituted additional regulations regarding the building of a synagogue. All of this was meant to ensure that the synagogue stand out among the other buildings in order to indicate its exalted status. These laws, which had been formulated in earlier generations and in the Land of Israel, later served as the guiding light for Jewish communities wherever they were, even at those times that the Jewish people was confronted by harsh decrees in the various places of its dispersion. Rabbi Joseph Caro, the author of the *Shulhan Arukh,* the universally accepted code of Jewish Law, repeats the provisions regarding the building of a synagogue and even adds more as Jewish communities added them over the generations.[5] To be more precise, the formulations laid down in the *Shulhan Arukh* reflect the religious rules that were the guiding light for the Jewish leaders in Spain, and it was from these traditions that he derived his rulings. It is thus obvious that the laws of the Mishnah, the *Tosefta*, and the Talmud underlie the codification by Rabbi Joseph Caro.

This is the stipulation in halakha (Jewish religious law) as to the location and status of the synagogue: "A synagogue may only be built at the highest place in the city, and it must be raised so as to stand higher than all the city homes that use it, as opposed to fortresses and towers that are not used. If a roof is sloped and cannot be used, one estimates

Decorative windows in the Shmuel HaLevi Abulafia synagogue in Toledo; a fine example of the Mudejar art in Spain.

up to which point it can be used, i.e., if there is an attic under the roof, it may not be higher than the synagogue." It also states: "If a person built a house higher than the synagogue, some say that we force him to lower it. If one built a high house and ensured that one corner is lower than the synagogue, that is sufficient."[6] These provisions could be enforced when the Jewish community was independent and able to impose its will upon all its members. The question is: to what extent did the Jews in Spain have the ability to enforce these laws?

Sometimes, the Jewish quarters or neighborhoods were at the lowest point in the town, as in a valley, and it followed that regardless of how the synagogue was built, it would remain relatively low as compared to the other buildings in the city. From this we can understand that the community leaders were able to abide by the provisions of Jewish law only in certain cases and were unable to deal with such factors which were beyond their control.[7]

Thus the community leaders took into account only their own neighborhoods, taking care to ensure that the synagogue was higher than all the houses of Jews in that area. Even in such cases there were sometimes deviations – when Jews managed to move beyond what had been their previous boundary and to build in areas which had been forbidden to them earlier. Since these new areas might well be on higher ground than that of the synagogue, thus it could happen that some houses were higher than the local synagogue. Generally, when that happened, the situation remained such that the synagogue was indeed lower than the Jews' homes. That, for example, was the case in Segovia, when the Jewish neighborhood moved to higher ground and the old synagogue still remained in the lower area. The question of houses being higher than the synagogue was a major problem in the synagogue built by Samuel ha-Levi Abulafia in Toledo. Abulafia's house, which he built to the east of the synagogue, was on higher ground than that of the synagogue.[8] Based on the structure of this house, it appears that they acted in accordance with Jewish law. Most of the wings of the house, with one exception, are only a single story and are lower than the synagogue to their west. The house also contains later additions from the time of El Greco, who lived in it about two hundred years later.

As to the height of the city's towers, gates, and fortresses, Jewish law had already dealt with the question and offered its own solution. All of those structures needed for the defense of the city were not included in the strictures against constructing a building higher than the synagogue, since they were not meant to be used as residences in the normal sense. Therefore, they were exempt from the strictures regarding maximum heights.

As to the height of the churches in relation to the synagogues, the Jews were obviously unable to intervene. Those who designed the churches and those who built them wanted to construct buildings that would stand out in their environs, and that would be especially true regarding the bell tower. Thus the cathedrals and the central churches, but also the neighborhood churches, stood out above the neighboring buildings. And even if the church as such did not tower over the other buildings, it would have a bell tower attached that would do so. The church authorities made sure to have the king's decree that the churches and their towers must always be higher than the synagogues. They also ensured that these rules would be observed even in those eras where the royal courts were liberal and where Jews enjoyed freedom of worship.

Even before the community leaders began to rack their brains about the synagogue's appearance and height, the first problem they faced was to find an area where it could be built. The Jewish areas were very limited in size, their population was large, and as a result there was serious overcrowding. To add to the space problem, locations had to be found for a synagogue and other communal buildings. This situation resulted in a great deal of tension and imposed solutions which were often grotesque and undesirable. This situation was nearly impossible to deal with, and the immediate solution was that in most cases they did not build large synagogues. Thus, very few large synagogues were constructed, and in most cases small synagogues were built for small groups. Sometimes they merely set side a room in a private home to be used as a synagogue. These constraints even affected the plans of the synagogues. That is how we are to understand the synagogue in Cordoba, which started off as a room in a private home, whose dimensions are no larger than that of a large room in a wealthy home, or even less than that. These objective difficulties, which affected all the residential Jewish quarters in the Spanish cities, dictated to the community leaders difficult solutions in planning the synagogues and in preserving their unique character and stateliness. There were certain essential conditions for a synagogue to function, such as light to read by during prayer or even study time, for many of the synagogues also served as study halls and schools and therefore needed sufficient light. The halakhic authorities thus determined that if one builds any other structure near the synagogue, it must be some distance from the synagogue walls and windows, so that the synagogue would be more readily discernible, as well as not to have any individual benefit from the communal property, and especially so that light would enter the building. This detail was even emphasized: "If one builds opposite the window of a synagogue, it is not enough to leave [only] four cubits (approximately two to three meters), as [the synagogue] needs a great deal of light."[9] However, the actual conditions did not always permit this provision to be fulfilled. In the synagogue in Seville, not only did they not leave a distance between the residences and the synagogue,

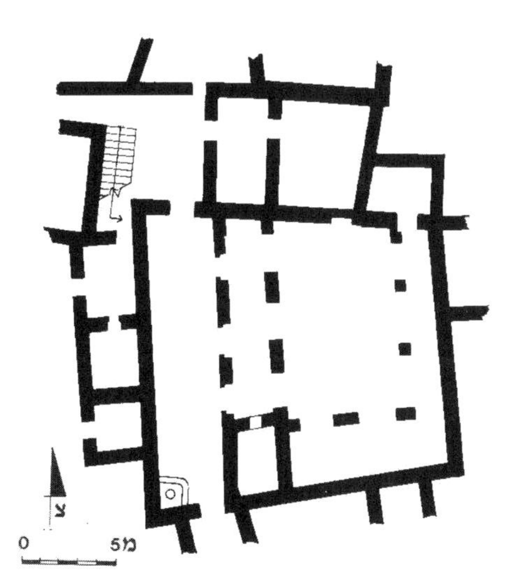

Ein Gedi, the plan of the synagogue and its auxiliary buildings.

but they also built homes on one of the wings. On the northern side of the synagogue hall they built residential rooms, and the same alongside the northern wall of that side and outside it. The residential quarters thus were attached to the building and enveloped it. Thus the windows on that side were blocked and light only entered the synagogue from the southern side (see the detailed description of the Seville synagogue, as well as the illustrations). One can thus see that sometimes the conditions in the field and difficult living conditions annulled the law about the synagogue, its dimensions, its appearance, and the way it was to function.

Although there is evidence that overcrowding had an adverse effect on the local synagogue and its surroundings, that was not the general rule. As a rule, the synagogue needed open space in its area. Several communal buildings – the study hall, the *mikveh*, assembly halls, and small halls – were all built close to the synagogue. Where the community was small and had limited financial resources, most of these functions were filled by the synagogue itself, with the main prayer hall and the women's section serving all these needs. In large cities, and especially in their central synagogues, there was no option other than to have a large courtyard or garden around the synagogue. All the other necessary public buildings were constructed in this courtyard. That was the case of the synagogues in Toledo. The synagogue of Cordoba – if it was not the private chapel of a wealthy individual but a regular synagogue and study hall – can serve as an example of a complex building, one part of which was a synagogue. In any event, the Cordoba synagogue could hold twenty to thirty people at most. The problem of overcrowding in the synagogues could be solved by having two consecutive services, one earlier and one later, thus doubling the number of worshippers.

The synagogues of Samuel ha-Levi and of Ibn Shoshan in Toledo had additional wings that served as study halls. Those who studied there regularly did not need to use the main prayer hall except for its unique functions. The synagogue of Samuel ha-Levi was found to have other rooms which served as a cloakroom, storage facilities, etc. Samuel ha-Levi, because of his excellent connections with the royal court, was able to receive a large tract of land for his synagogue, but this was not necessarily the case for other synagogues in Spain. Beyond the rooms attached to the synagogue, the building was surrounded by a courtyard enclosed by a sturdy wall. It was possible to use the courtyard as a prayer hall in the summer; to put up the *sukkah* each year, as required by each synagogue's regulations in those days; as well as to build a structure for a *mikveh*. As noted, the two Toledo synagogues had courtyards which are visible to this day while the other synagogues, because of changes made in the area, including the paving of roads along a different path from the one in existence when the area was a Jewish one, and other changes made in the intervening five hundred years, it is impossible to identify or locate the courtyards around the synagogues without a methodological study accompanied by excavations. We should note that in front of the market synagogue in Seville, a small public square was found several years ago. There is evidence to show that the vast majority of this square had been part of the synagogue courtyard. There are open areas and buildings in front of the Segovia synagogue, and on its northern side as well. It is possible that the courtyard and other public buildings were ancillary to the large synagogues.

Even when the builders of the synagogue had sufficient land, and all the more so when they only had a small plot, the plan had to call for a modest building. Add to this the government's stringent regulations regarding the synagogue's appearance and we can understand why the main architectural effort was expended on designing the interior. The Jews were fully aware that even if the law permitted them a grand exterior, and even if at the time the synagogue was being built the regime was more tolerant and liberal, they could not allow themselves to be deceived by circumstances and had to downplay the building's exterior. If the mere existence of a synagogue was a target for wild Christian mobs, egged on by their priests, why draw attention to the synagogue building and make it easier for the mob to find it? Furthermore, if the exterior was ornate, it might attract the attention of the secular government officials and especially the kings, who might reason that if the Jews had enough money to build so lavish a synagogue, surely greater taxes could be imposed on them! All these factors meant that the primary planning related to the interior, as in the words of the Biblical verse (Psalms 45:14): "The glory of the king's daughter is internal." Indeed, when that was the reality of the situation, they soon found ideological support for such a stand, especially since the architecture of the Arab mosques and of their palaces, which – for their own reasons – had subdued exteriors, while their interiors were a feast for the eyes. Thus, unlike the lavish interiors of the synagogues, the synagogue exteriors were merely practical and functional.

Jerusalem, the First Temple, plan, cross-section, and view.

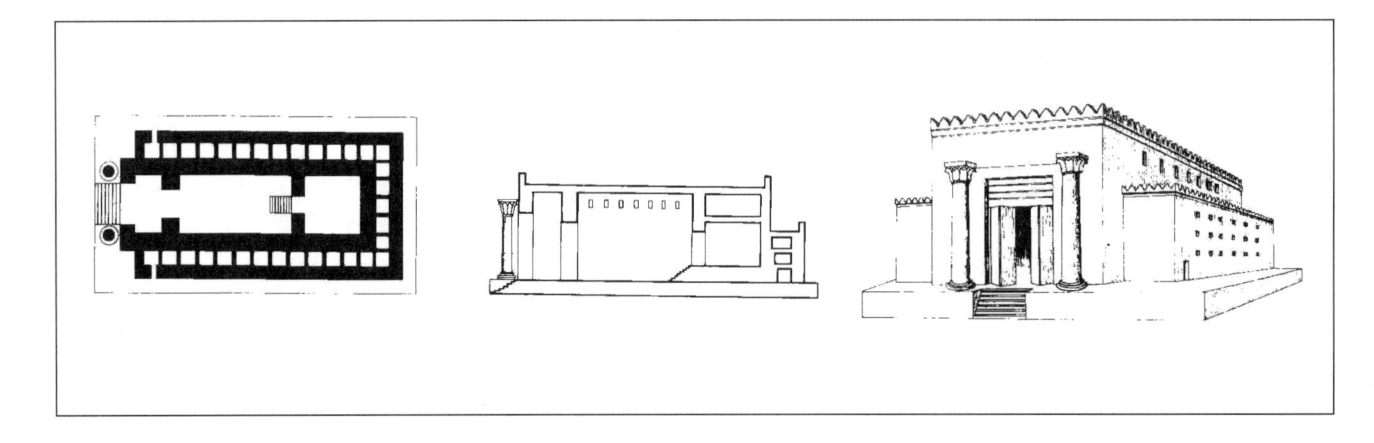

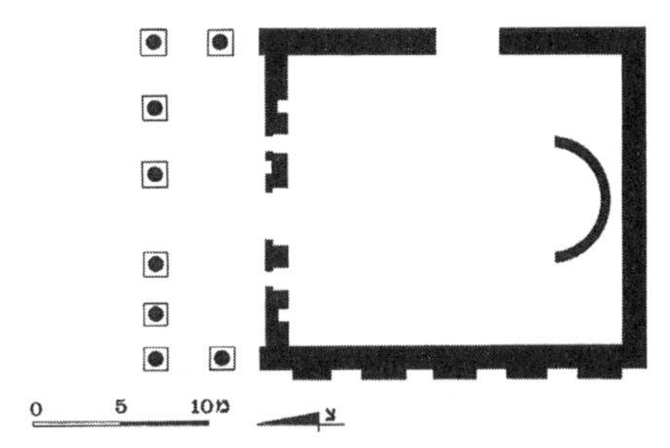

Kadesh in Galilee, the plan of a pagan temple.

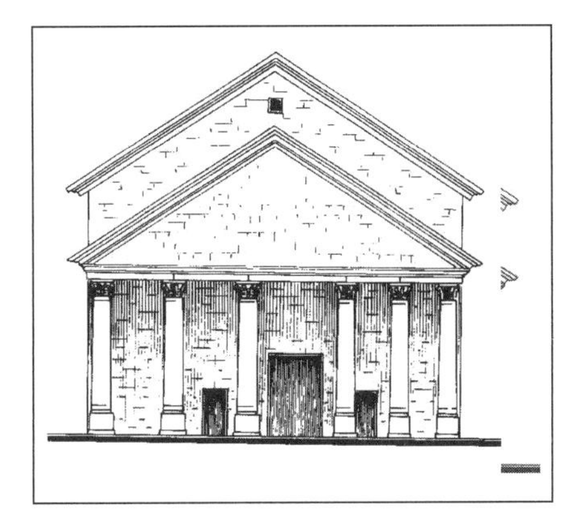

Kadesh in Galilee, reconstructed facade of the temple.

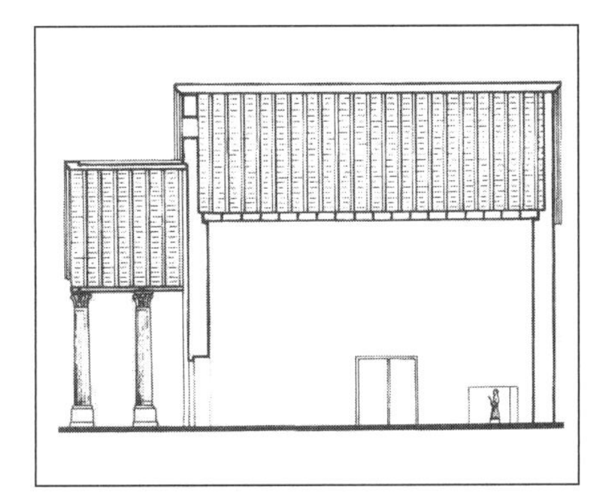

Kadesh in Galilee, reconstructed cross-section along the length of the temple. In the niche at the right was an idol of the god.

The Synagogue Plans and Buildings – Architecture and Construction – The Main Principles of the Plans

he temples of the ancient world served as homes for their gods. People live in beautiful homes, kings in palaces, and the gods obviously had to live in the most lavish of buildings – the temples. Only very few people – those who had special permission to do so – were allowed into the temples, and those who were permitted to enter them did so in order to offer services to the gods and to mediate between them and the people. The people themselves only entered the courtyards around the temples. However, when Judaism and, later on, Christianity needed to construct buildings for worship – which meant the entry of many people under one roof in order to hold the ritual – the original temple plans of the other nations could not serve as a model. A plan was needed that would be appropriate for the required function. The synagogue and the church thus drew inspiration for their plans from the basilica, a Greco-Roman building that had served for civil purposes and whose plans were derived from that need. The basilica contained most of the city's courts. Money-changers had their businesses there, and major financial transactions were conducted there. Thus, every self-respecting city built itself a basilica, which had a forum, or business center. The basilica could hold a large number of people, which made it suitable for gathering places such as the synagogue and the church, which arose later on and required halls that could hold large gatherings, and was ornate as well.

The primary layout of a basilica is rectangular. The hall is divided into three units by means of two rows of pillars running along its length. This division, which split the hall into three units, was essential, for otherwise it would have been impossible to house the entire space under a single roof, as it is very difficult to obtain wood beams that are long enough and strong enough to traverse the entire width of the space.[10] Even though this was the prototype for their synagogue plans, we do not find that it was adhered to uncompromisingly. In the synagogues of the Byzantine era in the Land of Israel, and especially in those of the fifth to the seventh centuries C.E., we find some basilica buildings that are elongated, while others are almost square. The plans are similar, but not identical.[11] Later the basilica model was broadened, so that there were four pillars instead of two. This allowed for a central hall and two additional halls on each side of the central one. This added considerably to the area of the prayer hall and allowed for the possibility of using the side units for other purposes.

In the Spanish synagogues, it appears that the basilica plan was very common. Thus we find a basilica with five units in the Ibn Shoshan synagogue in Toledo, three-unit basilicas in Segovia and in Seville, as well as in a number of other buildings in other cities. Along with the basilica, we also find a single hall without any pillars dividing it into separate units, as in the Samuel ha-Levi synagogue in Toledo. An analysis of the plans of this structure can also show us that it was constructed with three areas, but they were divided by walls rather than by pillars. The prayer area was a single rectangular hall that was not divided up into sections. The plan of the Cordoba synagogue is exceptional, but one cannot evaluate it in terms of the plans of synagogues elsewhere, for what we have there is a normal room which was converted into a synagogue. There are scholars who regard this as a lateral structure, with which we are acquainted from other synagogues in Italy and other places.[12] This hypothesis is incorrect, and those who proposed it analyzed this synagogue based only on its plans.

In the plans of the synagogues in the Land of Israel under the Byzantine rule, which were based on the basilica and which are recognized as synagogue plans from later times or from the Middle Ages, a niche is built into the wall facing Jerusalem. This semicircular niche usually protruded from the building wall. In rare instances it was sunk into the wall and did not protrude. This niche was meant to contain the Holy Ark, in which the Torah scrolls were kept. In the Spanish synagogues, the apse did not extend beyond the building line. The Holy Ark, which held the Torah scrolls, was generally a solid structure which was part of the building, adjacent to the eastern wall, the "Jerusalem wall" in Europe, including Spain. It was generally a rectangular structure, sometimes with a window above it facing the outside. In such cases, when the doors of the Holy Ark were opened during the prayer service and the congregants looked eastward, they would see the blue sky and the east.

As noted, most Holy Arks were rectangular, although in the Seville synagogue the Holy Ark was in a semi-circular niche, as was the norm in the synagogues in the Land of Israel. This may have been the case in Segovia too. The reason such niches did not extend outside the building wall in Spain might have been because of the demands of the Church, which did not want any other building to look like the Christian churches. This might have been the thought of those who planned the synagogues, who did not want to offer any hints as to the purpose of the building to anyone outside it because of their fear that mobs might attack the building and the Jews.

Three types of pillars supported the roofing of the synagogue and separated the various areas: round pillars such as those in the synagogue in Seville, octagonal pillars such as those in Segovia and in the Ibn Shoshan synagogue in Toledo, and square pillars in some of the small synagogues. The tops of the pillars were decorated with carvings of flora or of geometric patterns. They never used figures of

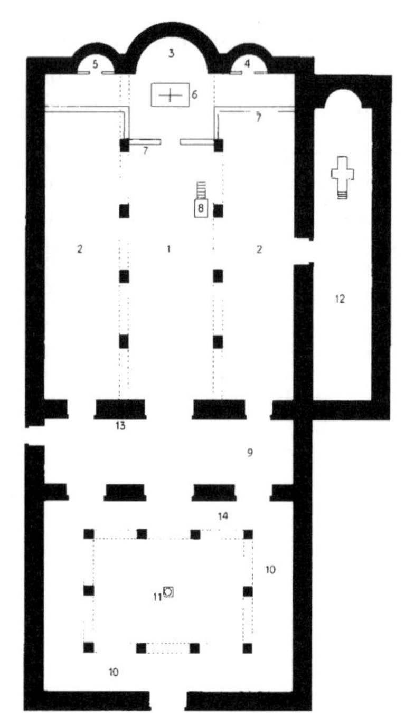

A typical plan of a Byzantine-era church in the Land of Israel: 1) the central hall; 2) side halls; 3) Synthronon (the joint bench); 4) room to prepare the Holy Wafers; 5) Diaconicon (dressing room); 6) Presybterium (the sanctified area and the altar); 7) mesh or weave; 8) Ambo - where the preacher stood; 9) Narthex - waiting room; 10) Porches around the courtyard; 11) Atrium; 12) Baptistry; 13) Facade from the west, with three entrances; 14) Facade for entry into the Narthex, with three entrances.

Jerusalem, Temple Mount, the basilica. Reconstruction of a cross-section of the breadth of the building, above the area known as Solomon's Stables.

Typical examples of the eastern wall of churches in the Byzantine era in the Land of Israel: 1) a round central niche which protrudes outside;
2) three niches all of which are inside the church building; 3) three round niches protruding outward from the eastern wall; 4) a round central niche with a rectangular room on each side of it; 5) a round niche and two round niches west of it in the shape of a clover leaf.

Jerusalem, Temple Mount, the basilica, reconstruction and a view into the building space.

animals or people even though such figures were very common in church architecture in Spain at the time. Between the pillars were arches made of stone or bricks. The tops of these all ended in a unified line at the height of the top of the upper arch. (?) On this line, the building extended upward, (?) whether as a line of windows or as a solid wall meant to support the roof. Unlike the basilica in the Land of Israel and sometimes even in the ancient Christian ones in Spain, there were no wooden beams between the pillars along the length of the pillar, but they always constructed arches between one pillar and the next in order to form a base for the continued construction.

The arches were sometimes round, as in Seville, but in general they were horseshoe-shaped arcs, which were typical of Spanish Muslim architecture and later of Christian architecture in the Iberian peninsula. This is most apparent in the Ibn Shoshan, Segovia, and Caceres synagogues. Sometimes the arch was not smooth on the inner side, but was constructed and decorated with ornate waves, a device that imparts a feeling of majesty and great embellishment to the arch.

The decorations of these and of the capitals of the pillars, as well as the decorations on the walls and of the arches, were all carried out in accordance with the prevalent style in Spain at that time, the Mudejar style. The Mudejar architecture was one planned by Muslims, who functioned under the Christian rule but according to the finest Muslim traditions.[13] The Toledo synagogues are among the most classic and beautiful examples of this style in Spain.

In the basilica buildings, both of the churches and of the synagogues, the main entrance to the main hall and to the side halls was generally in the wall parallel to the wall that had the niche: the western wall, which is a transverse wall. Almost without exception, that was the case for the synagogues of the Byzantine era in the Land of Israel up to the seventh century C.E., and so too for the ruins of synagogues of which we are aware from later eras.[14]

In the Spanish synagogues there was a substantive change from this formula, with the entrance no longer in the transverse wall. If we do find entrances in the western wall, there is no guarantee that they were there originally, for they might have been added later in addition to the main entrance on the northern or southern wall. Although the entrance was sometimes situated at the end of the longitudinal wall, close to the western wall, it was usually located in the middle of the longitudinal wall. It is not clear what caused the moving of the entrance to the longitudinal wall. It is possible that this hints at a change in one of the focal points in the synagogue. We have reason to assume that the *tevah* or *bimah*, which was used, among others, for the Torah reading, was moved to the western wall at the other end of the synagogue, opposite the Holy Ark at the eastern wall. This meant that it was no longer possible to have the entrance in the western wall, so

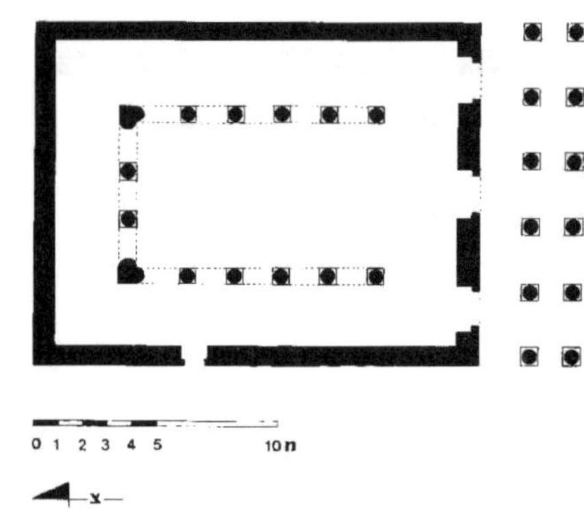

Bar'am, plan of the synagogue and the porch in front of it.

Bar'am, southern facade of the synagogue, reconstructed view.

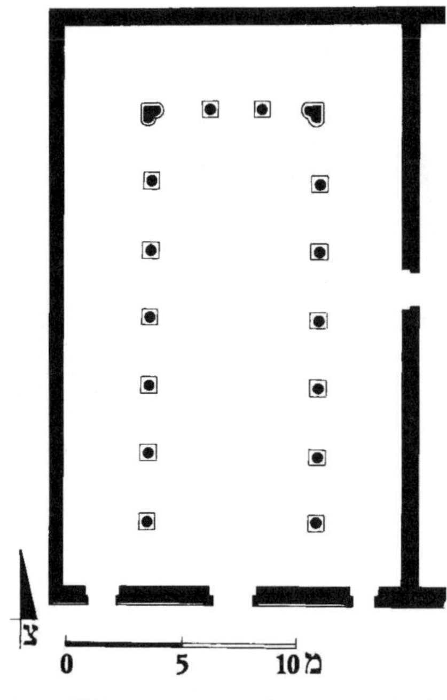

Beit Alfa, synagogue plan; prayer hall, waiting room and courtyard.

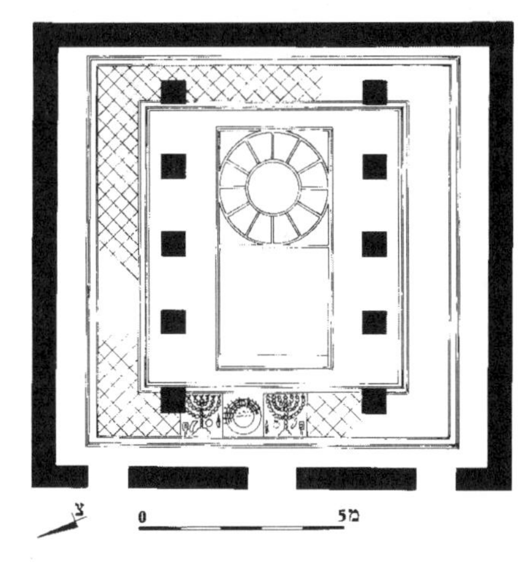

Usifiyyah, plan of the synagogue in the Jewish town of Hosifah.

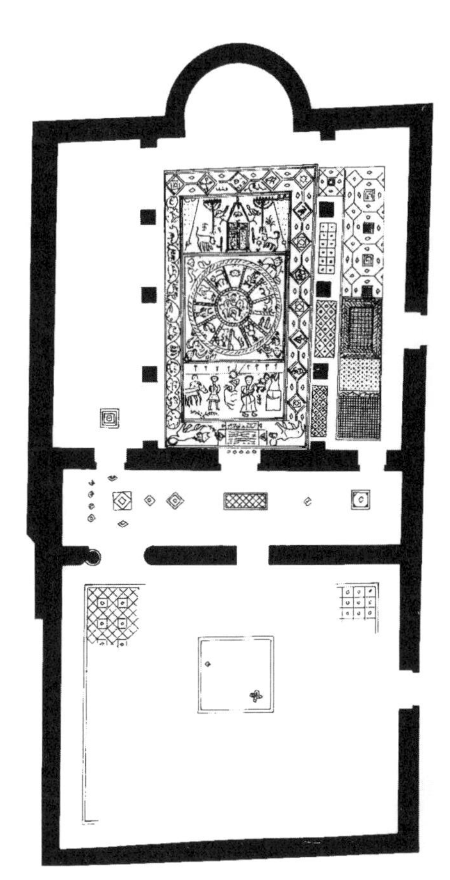

Beit Alfa, synagogue plan; prayer hall,waiting room and courtyard.

the entrance had to be situated in one of the longitudinal walls. That way, the worshippers could enter the synagogue without ascending immediately to the *tevah*.

As noted earlier, in the Ibn Shoshan synagogue in Toledo and in the Seville synagogue there are also entrances on the western side, but we do not know whether these were added later, when the buildings were converted into churches. As for the Ibn Shoshan synagogue, if the western entrance was indeed part of the original plan, it is possible that this was an entry foyer to the women's section. We should note that in the Segovia synagogue, even though it serves today as a church, only the original entrance remains: the one on the northern side, and there is no entrance on the western side. It is possible that this is a consequence of the building's reconstruction in the twentieth century after a fire. At the time of its reconstruction, there was already an awareness of the subject of synagogues in Spain, and those who reconstructed the building decided to do so according to what it had been as a synagogue and to seal off the western entrance that it had used when it served as a church until the mid-twentieth century.[15]

The Spanish synagogues, at least those which are still standing, show us that in addition to the main structure there were a number of attached wings, some built along with the main building and others added at a later time. Some of them were essential for the conducting of the synagogue affairs, and others were such that the synagogue could function without them.

One of the classic characteristics of the Spanish synagogues was a separate entrance hall. Generally, the entrance to the synagogue was through an entrance on a longitudinal wall, i.e., from the side. After entering through the door, one entered a small room which was separate from the central hall. To move from this room to the main hall, one had to pass through another locked door. This room served as a cloakroom for hanging up coats, and so on. It also contained the *maskilta*, a basin for washing one's hands before entering the prayer hall.[16] This room served primarily as a transition from the profane to the sacred, as one entered from the outside world. In those synagogues where there was only a single hall without side halls, the entrance room was constructed in a side wing of the building. Thus, for example, in the synagogue of Samuel ha-Levi Abulafia in Toledo, as well as in the small synagogue in Cordoba, the entrance hall is under the women's section.

In those synagogues whose plans are like that of a basilica, the cloakroom is on the side closest to the wall where the entrance to the synagogue lies. Sometimes this room, which is some distance from the side, contains a stairway to the women's section. This room was sometimes built of hard materials, while other times it was built of wood. That was the case, for example, in the large synagogue in Segovia.

In that case, the women's section is located above the cloakroom at the western end of the synagogue building. It is possible that the Ibn Shoshan synagogue in Toledo had the same type of entrance as well, but the entrance to that room and from there to the women's section was through an entrance that was originally located in the western wall rather than on the northern or southern longitudinal wall. As noted above, the cloakroom also had the stairway that led to the women's section, but when it was a large building and space permitted, they built a separate cloakroom for women, which also contained the staircase to the women's section. That, for example, was the case in the Samuel ha-Levi synagogue in Toledo, which had a cloakroom for men in the southwestern wing, whereas a separate entrance and cloakroom was constructed for women in the southeastern wing, from which a staircase led to the women's section.

Several sources indicate that the synagogue building complex also included a study hall and a school for young children (what would later be called a *heder* in the Ashkenazic communities). There were cases where the synagogue had a large wing that served as a yeshivah or study hall where young men studied and where, on occasion, they even lived. In some synagogues in Spain we found that what has remained to this day is primarily the synagogue itself, but there are hints that classrooms were attached to it, as was the case in the Samuel ha-Levi synagogue in Toledo. In this building the northern wing, with its three vaulted rooms, served as a study hall, including classrooms. Obviously, it is possible that these rooms were used as the offices of the community rabbi and as courtrooms for the community and the rabbi. These adjacent rooms were also used for other activities connected to the community's needs and lifestyle, such as preparing a young man for his *bar mitzvah.*

Ideally, to learn the functions that the wings in the synagogue courtyard filled, one should study the buildings in the courtyard of the Cordoba synagogue. Yet since these buildings now serve as private homes, at present such a study is impossible. Another possibility is to study the large synagogue in Segovia, but there the entire structure, including the adjacent rooms, is used as a Christian church and monastery, the Corpus Christi, and such a study has not been possible until this time. What is more interesting and encouraging is the picture that emerges from the synagogue in the Seville market. There, in the northern wing, are private residential homes that were built on the northern side of the synagogue. The question with which the present study will deal is whether these homes were originally used as private residences or whether they were originally rooms and apartments of the synagogue, such as a study hall, the rabbi's chambers, his apartment, and so on. One should note that in Europe it was customary to have the rabbi's apartment adjacent to and attached to the synagogue. That was the case in Venice and in Lübeck, Germany, and in many other cities.

In the Jewish quarters which have been discovered in the cities of Barcelona, Gerona, Lucerne, and others, *mikva'ot* were also found, but not quite adjacent to the synagogues. It would be logical to assume that originally they were near the synagogue and in one of the wings adjacent to it, and that there was some physical link between the synagogue and the *mikveh*. These places, too, await someone to redeem them and to investigate and analyze their hidden mysteries, for what is visible is but a fraction of that which still waits to be discovered, and the answers to the myriad questions about them are buried deep in the ground in the vicinity of the synagogue.

Pinkerfeld pointed out the connection between the existence of *mikva'ot* in Jewish communities and synagogues, and it is appropriate to investigate this in Spain as well.[17] Sometimes *mikva'ot* were found in the cellars underneath the synagogues, and the entrance to the *mikveh*

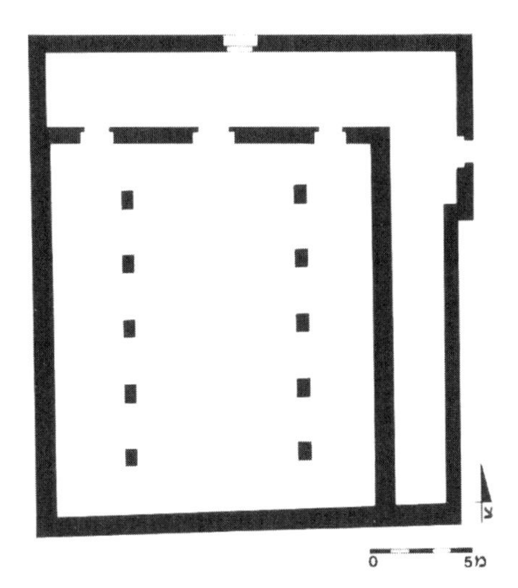

Rehov, synagogue plan and waiting rooms at its front and side.

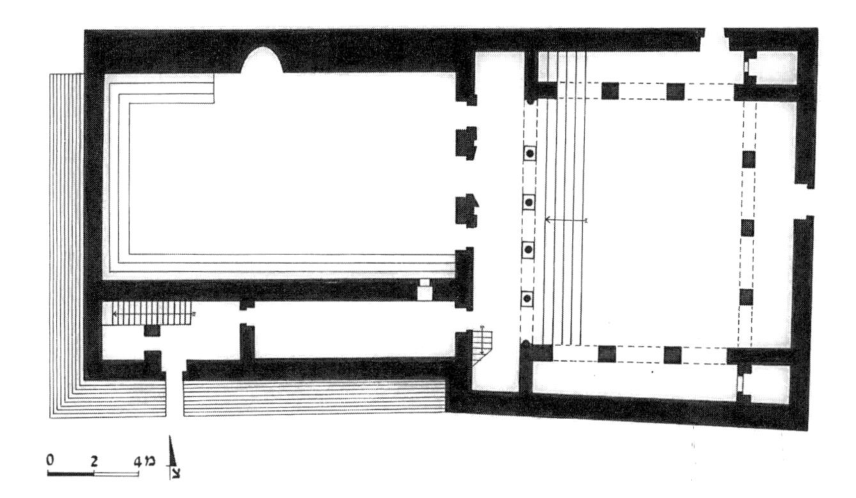

▶ Hurvat Sussiya, synagogue plan. In the east, the entrance hall and in front of it a courtyard and porch around it.

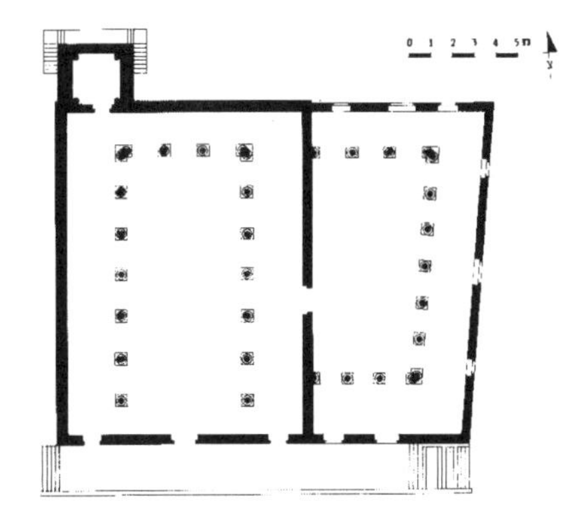

▼ Capernaum, synagogue plan, and the courtyard and side aisles to its east.

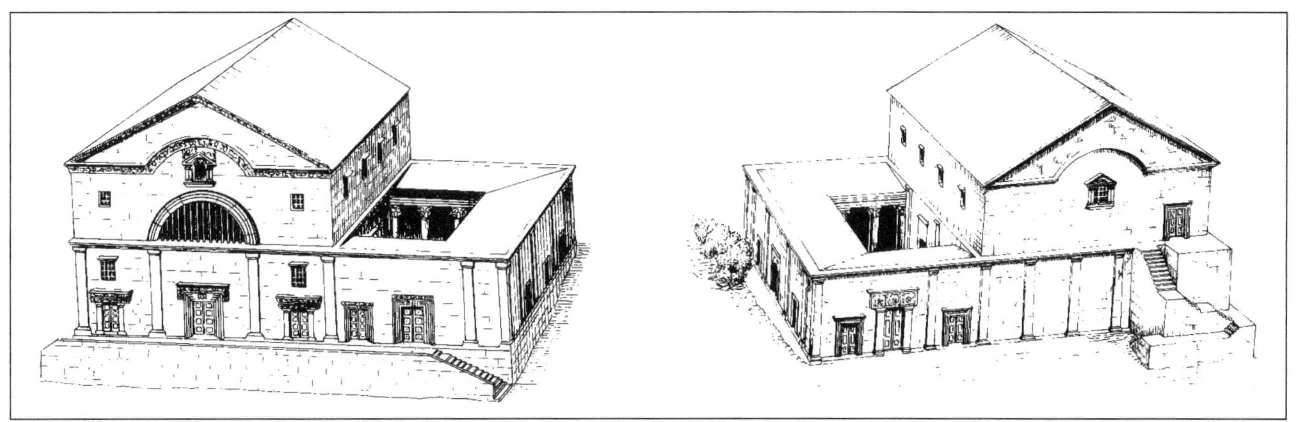

▼ Capernaum, reconstruction and perspective view of the front of the synagogue

▼ Capernaum, reconstruction and perspective view of the rear of the synagogue and the steps to the women's section

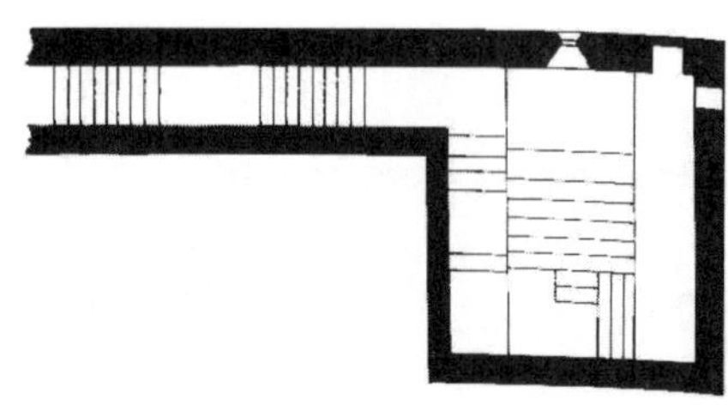

▲ Basalo, *mikveh*, plan.

◀ Basalo, *mikveh*, perspective view to the descent into the *mikveh.*

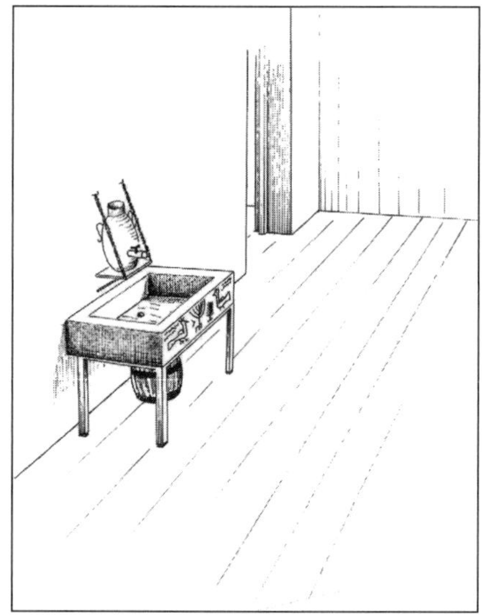

Proposed reconstruction of the *maskilta*, the basin in the synagogue waiting room.

Maskilta, basin for washing the hands before prayer. Found in Spain, decorated with the text, *Shalom al Yisrael* – "Peace on Israel"

was sometimes from the synagogue hall or from the courtyard, close to it.[18]

To study the wings of the synagogues in Spain properly, one needs to examine the secular construction related to it. Here we refer to the stores and workshops that were adjacent to the synagogues. In Spain, there is still one extant example of this, namely the synagogue of the market in Seville, Santa Maria la Blanca. The importance of this topic lies in the fact that it can show us the how the communities financed synagogue upkeep – funding that did not depend only on the collection of money from individuals and that was available independently to the synagogue wardens and the public coffers. Such practices were common in ancient temples as well as in the Second Temple in Jerusalem. The numerous stores in the Temple squares and in the streets adjacent to the Temple Mount were the property of the priesthood, which rented them out and used the rental money to finance the Temple's needs.[19]

Such a tradition may be found among the Muslims as well. Almost every urban mosque, including the large and important ones, owns secular property, generally stores, whose rental finances the mosque's needs.[20] This was also the practice in the Christian world in the Land of Israel, and was especially true during the period of Crusader rule.[21]

It appears that such methods are among the best and most acceptable ways to promote the independent economic existence of religious institutions. It is therefore worthwhile to investigate and examine the practice of the synagogues in Spain, both architecturally and in terms of historical documentation.

The Walls and Construction Materials

The Spanish synagogues were built of materials that were in common use in Spain at that time. Even though many private buildings used wood as the primary building material, those who constructed public buildings preferred more enduring materials that could withstand fires. That was why the walls were built primarily of unhewn stone or fire-hardened bricks. Sometimes, the building was constructed of two materials, both stone and bricks. Building with either of these materials required excellent mortar that was rich in lime, which served as a binder, and indeed that was what was used in the building of the synagogues' walls.[22] In those days, the construction of cathedrals and churches primarily used hewn stone, granite, soft and hard limestone and, rarely, marble. It is indeed possible to find small churches in the small towns and village of Europe built of brick, but in the large cities they generally used ornate hewn stone.[23]

Until now, we have not found any synagogues in Spain built of hewn stone, and it is not known why this was so. Could it be because hewn stone was expensive? Was it by governmental decree, so that the synagogues should not look attractive? Another possibility, which has already been raised in a different context, is that this was a voluntary decision by the Jewish community in order not to arouse the envy of the non-Jews or draw the government's attention to the community's financial state. See above regarding the design of the synagogues in general.

Sometimes the outer walls of the synagogues were coated with a thick coating of clay and whitewashed, as were the other buildings in the town, and the synagogue was simply "swallowed up" among its neighboring houses. Sometimes, before the clay dried, lines were drawn in it with a ruler to make it look like a stone wall. This device was also prevalent in private homes. When a building was constructed of unhewn stone, its corners were built of hewn stone. This was done because construction that way is much easier.

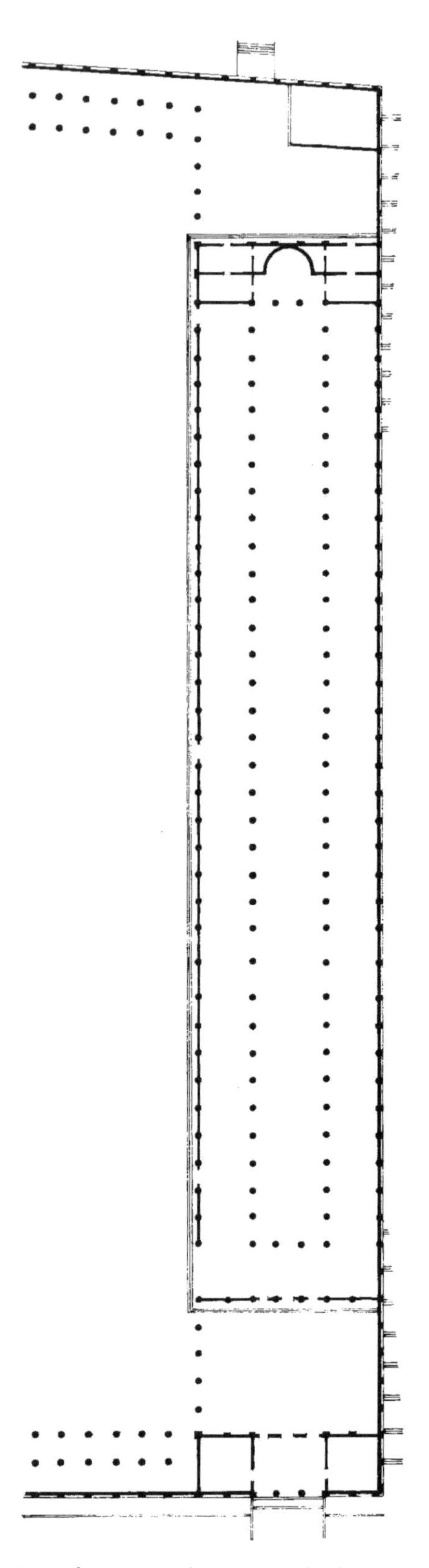

Jerusalem, Temple Mount, the basilica, plan

Floors, Ceilings, and Roofs

he Jews' living conditions among a hostile Christian population gave rise to a tradition that the only decoration and adornment of the synagogue was in the synagogue hall. Because of the constraints that compelled this type of planning and construction, an ideology developed that this was the proper Jewish way. In any case, we have a situation where synagogue interiors were ornate while the exteriors were simple. These principles were also in keeping with the concepts prevalent in both religious and secular Muslim architecture, which at that time was also based primarily on the decoration of the interior. However, the Muslim architects did not neglect the exterior as much as the Jewish architects did. For example, the large mosque in Cordoba had external walls with breathtaking decorations. As to residential buildings, the Muslims made a point of keeping their exteriors modest, whereas their interiors were lavish. That was the case with the Alhambra in Granada and the Alcazar in Seville.

As to the churches in Spain, until the end of the first millennium C.E. the churches there had very simple exteriors with the primary decorations on the inside. Beginning with the second millennium in the eleventh and twelfth centuries and increasingly thereafter, the appearance of the outer wall of the church building and especially the front wall was upgraded until it eventually became full of art works. This was the exact opposite of the position of the Jewish architects in Spain. The extravagant Christian exteriors in Spain were influenced by what was happening at the time in the other European states, and Spain did not lag behind them. It may also have been the Christian reaction to their liberation from the Arabic-Muslim yoke and their joy at the establishment of a free Christian state. Under Islam, the Christians had been very modest in decorating their churches, as the Jews had been under Christian rule. However, when the Christians were freed from Muslim domination, they gave expression to what they regarded as the superiority of their religion and their freedom in decorating the exteriors of their churches in a way that would attract the attention of all.

The internal architecture of the Spanish synagogues encountered a major problem. The building, which had never been particularly high for the reasons noted above, presented difficulties to the planners. Every addition to the height of the synagogue improved it, both in terms of making the inside look better and in meeting the need for a balcony for the women, as well as the need to have sufficient air for a large number of worshippers even when the windows were shuttered.

One of the solutions found in some of the synagogues was that the synagogue floor was lower than ground level, sometimes more than half a meter (about twenty inches) lower. In other cases, the floor was at ground level, but usually never higher than that. The sunken level helped a little in terms of the building's height. However, this solution added no luster to the building, as the general rule was that one should ascend to holy places – this was especially so in the Temple in Jerusalem, but also in several synagogues in the Galilee in Mishnaic and Talmudic times. It is clear that in order to enter Christian holy places one had to climb a number of steps. Here too, where one did not have to climb any steps in order to enter the synagogue, an ideology was found to justify it, based on Psalms 130:1: "Out of the depths I called to You, O Lord," i.e., that the place from which one prays should be low, with the worshippers praying submissively and bent humbly before God.[24] This idea of lowering the floor of the synagogue because of the foreign domination under which the Jews lived later became a tradition. One finds echoes of this in the architecture of synagogues in Poland and even in the Land of Israel under Ottoman rule.

Sometimes, in order to create an impression of striving upward, in order for the synagogue to tower over its immediate vicinity, they added a long, thin steel rod that was not particularly noticeable but added something, at least as a way to express their desire for the synagogue to be high. This was nevertheless a concession to the hostile Christian environment. It was found in Germany,[25] but we do not have sufficient information to know whether this tradition had originated in Spain and migrated to Germany after the expulsion from Spain. Without going into detail, it would appear that this was the case. The German synagogues drew a great deal from the architecture of the Spanish synagogues and from their practices and customs.

One of the substantive problems faced by those who planned the synagogue halls in terms of the height of the hall was the women's section, as this upper balcony raised the height of the hall. Indeed, on occasion they did not build the women's section in the upper balcony, but set aside a place for it in one of the side sections of the building, at the same level as the main prayer hall. That was the case where it was impossible to construct buildings to the desired height, such as, for example, in the Ibn Shoshan synagogue in Toledo, which was originally on a plot which was higher than its surroundings and where it was impossible to build it to the desired height. They were thus forced to do without an upper balcony for the women's section.

In this regard we should mention the great cathedral in Toledo and the Church of Saint John of the Catholic monarchs, which were built in the heart of the Jewish quarter. In both cases, one must climb down a number of steps from ground level to enter them, and there is a basis for the tradition that both were built on the sites of large synagogues that were seized from their owners.[26]

The floors of the Spanish synagogues were simple. In most cases they were constructed of stone or hardened brick. The bricks were generally laid like paving stones, in a straight line, but on occasion they were laid diagonally in order to break the straight line in relationship to the building walls and to vary the floor decoration somewhat. At other times they were laid in various patterns. In reality, this was not of great importance, because the floors were covered by carpets or at least mats, and the worshippers never saw the floors. The use of carpets and mats helped to create a warm atmosphere in the building and of course added the decoration that they desired.

When the women's section was located on a balcony, the floor was generally made of wood. In reality, the entire balcony was made of wood that had been brought into the prayer hall. The women's sections were sometimes used for classrooms or study halls.[27]

A great deal of attention in the women's section was paid to the ceiling of the synagogue. It was made of choice wood that had been treated and carved, and was a significant part of the building space. Above the ceiling was a roof, generally with a steep slope in order to ensure the proper and speedy flow of rainwater and to prevent it from accumulating, particularly as in the winter it could also snow. When snow melts, it needs a steep slope so that its weight will not press on the roof and leave puddles of water as it melts. When water remains on the roof it eventually seeps into the building and penetrates the walls, eventually bringing about the destruction of the interior decorations. In some cases it causes the entire structure to weaken and even to collapse eventually. Sloping roofs are a common sight in European construction in general, including in Spain. When one constructs a building with a sloping roof, its ceiling is often nevertheless straight. Sometimes, the space between the ceiling and the roof is used as a storage area. If it is a public building such as a synagogue, the space may be used as a *genizah*, a storage area for various documents and written materials.

Although Spanish synagogues had sloping ceilings rather than straight ones, the builders encased the sloping lines with wood. The space therefore appeared in its full slope. (? – 46). By building in this way, a significant amount of height was added to the hall space, as much as a few meters (or yards). The additional height was clearly important: where the planner was limited in terms of the outer height of the building and of the roof, any addition to the height of the internal hall was significant. Therefore, the builders were very careful in laying the horizontal beams that supported the roof gables. These beams were works of art, and on occasion they had artistic elements carved into them. In addition to their utilitarian use in the building, they also served to decorate it. One of the beautiful examples is to be found in the Samuel ha-Levi Abulafia synagogue in Toledo.

The building roof was covered by fire-hardened clay tiles. Sometimes the tiles could be seen from inside the building, above the wooden support beams, and sometimes finished wooden planks were laid between the beams to hide the tiles. This created an artistically finished wooden partition which blocked off the tiles and fit in well with the ceiling beams and the roof.

The tiles were of a style commonly used in private homes. This helped greatly in ensuring that the synagogue blended in with the housing in the area.

The Women's Section

The study of ancient synagogues in the Land of Israel during the Mishnaic and Talmudic eras evidently shows us that there was a women's section in a raised balcony in the synagogue hall. This was already noted by Heinrich Kohl and Carl Watzinger in their descriptions and reconstructions of the ancient synagogues in the Galilee.[28] One should note that the ancient synagogues in the Land of Israel were found in an advanced state of ruin, and the idea of a women's gallery is based on what the

Capernaum, reconstruction and perspective view of the synagogue interior toward the southern wall

researchers knew of European synagogues of the past several centuries – specifically, the synagogues in their own countries, Germany and Czechoslovakia. It is clear that could not have proposed their hypothesis without some supporting data that the synagogues built in a basilica form contained some type of balcony. The hypothesis about an upper balcony in the synagogue structures is also based on the discovery of stairwells to an upper floor, as well as the uncovering of smaller pillars than those in the central hall, as found in the ruins of the buildings. These shorter pillars show us that there were additional columns of pillars above the pillar columns in the lower hall, which hint at the existence of a balcony. One must add to this the existence of larger pillars in the corners of the lower hall. These clearly show the existence of a balcony. If there was indeed an upper balcony in the synagogue, why would it not be for the use of the women, as we found in the synagogues in the Middle Ages? This is the logical conclusion.

The Hebrew term for the women's section, *ezrat nashim* (literally "women's courtyard"), is taken from the Second Temple era.[29] One should note that the *ezrat nashim* on the Temple Mount was used by both men and women, but only men were permitted to continue to the next courtyard. When the Temple stood, at the time of the *Simhat Bet ha-Sho'evah* celebration during the *Sukkot* holiday, women were not permitted to enter the *ezrat nashim* because of concern for modesty, but could stand on the roofs of the various chambers surrounding it, from which they could watch the proceedings.[30] From this the rabbis

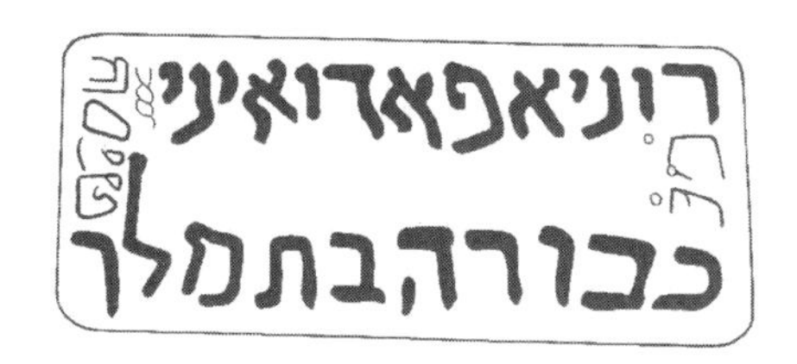

Inscription in Spain, "Donia Padoini, honor of the queen," indicating the status of Jewish women in Spain.

derived the concept of separating the men from the women by giving the women an upper balcony.

Shmuel Safrai questioned the existence of a balcony for women in the ancient synagogues in the Land of Israel.[31] We should note that his research and proposals do not disagree with the research and views of the many scholars who claimed that a there was women's section in the upper balcony of the synagogues during Mishnaic and Talmudic times. In any event, from the beginning of the second millennium C.E., the Spanish synagogues definitely contained an upper balcony that was used as a women's section, as did the Ezra ha-Sofer synagogue in Egypt during the ninth century C.E.[32] The synagogues in Italy,[33] Eastern Europe and Germany[34] had women's balconies. An exception was the synagogue in Worms, Germany, which dates back to the beginning of the second millennium, and some even say that this is the synagogue where Rashi prayed.[35] Without going into whether this is true, there is no doubt that this is an ancient synagogue. In this synagogue, the women's section is not in an upper balcony, but is almost at the same level as the men's section. What is unique here is that the women's section is in the same hall as that of the men and is linked to it. Here the division is minimal and there is no upper balcony.

In the Spanish synagogues there were some women's sections in the balconies, i.e., one flight up, but also others at ground level, separate from the main prayer hall – that of the men – but connected to it with minimal separation rather than in a separate balcony. Sometimes the women's section had a separate entrance. Indeed, both types of women's sections existed, and there was no iron-clad rule that the women's section had to be in a raised balcony. Even when the women's section was on ground level, on the same level as the men's section, there was a separate entrance for the women. Can we conclude from this that one of the sides included a rigid separation in order to separate the men and the women completely? We cannot provide an unequivocal answer to that question, but can only emphasize that where there was

Women's section at the same height as central prayer hall.

a women's section in the balcony in Sephardic synagogues, there was a great deal of liberalism regarding the exposure of women there. We should also add that when there was a separate balcony for women, they sometimes built a separate entrance for women, as in the Samuel ha-Levi synagogue in Toledo, while in other synagogues there was a common entrance for both men and women, as in the synagogue in the old section of Segovia. As noted, in the Ibn Shoshan synagogue in Toledo, because of the problem of height, it appears that they did not have a women's balcony, and they thus had a side aisle of the main hall for women, with a separate entrance. It is true that in this synagogue, too, one can reconstruct a balcony, but it would be of very modest dimensions.

Raised women's section.

In those synagogues that had women's balconies and that still exist, the railing was relatively low, about seventy centimeters (twenty-eight inches). The railing had woven wooden strips or plaster panels that were made to look like such strips, and more was revealed than was concealed. The women in the balcony had an excellent view of the entire service. For their part, the men could see the women in all their splendid clothing and beauty. Thus, the women could both see and be seen. While this tradition, with its ancient roots,[36] has continued among the Oriental Jews in most places,[37] it has not done so in most Ashkenazic communities. In their case, the partition was much higher and gradually became more and more opaque until the main hall of the synagogue became a place of mystery where the women could not see or be seen at all. They could only hear, and sometimes they could stand on chairs in order to see what was happening.[38]

In the Spanish synagogues, a great deal of attention was given to decorating and beautifying the women's section, inside and out, as it faced the main prayer hall. The decorations, which consisted of stucco in all kinds of geometric and floral patterns, were in keeping with the best of the tradition and style of decorating synagogues in general. The borders surrounding these decorations consisted of Biblical verses in Hebrew letters (see the section on decorations and inscriptions below). The verses selected for this related to women. For example, they might use the Song of Miriam, Moses's sister, at the Sea of Reeds or the text of Proverbs 31 (the "Woman of Valor" chapter).

In the Spanish Jewish communities women were respected and honored and enjoyed a great deal of freedom, not only in terms of the community affairs but also in dealing with the non-Jewish governmental authorities. Not even Jewish women in the Second Temple era or in the Land of Israel of the Mishnaic and Talmudic times had attained such high status. One can find details about the status of the Jewish women in Spain in various historical sources and even in archaeological epigraphic sources such as tombstones and in stone dedication tablets.[39] Scholars who study Spanish Jewry have devoted very little of their research to the history of the communities, and this topic still requires study.[40] Since the women were so respected and honored, it is not surprising that the women's section was decorated so lavishly. Even though Spanish Jewry followed tradition in keeping the men and women separate during prayers, they took pains to beautify the women's section. The Jewish expression that "the honor of the king's daughter lies in privacy" (Psalms 45:13) served to guide the architecture of the synagogues and their women's sections, but the architects emphasized "the king's daughter" and "honor" rather than "privacy."

Entrances, Doors, and Windows

In the Spanish synagogues, the entrance to the prayer hall was in one of the longitudinal walls, mostly in the southern wall but occasionally in the northern wall. The transverse walls were the eastern wall, also known as the "Jerusalem wall" – the heart of the synagogue – and its opposite wall, the western wall. This was the exact opposite of what was customary in the synagogues of the Land of Israel in Mishnaic and Talmudic times, excavations of which have revealed that the "Jerusalem wall" was not always the eastern wall. On the contrary – in the north of the country it was the southern wall and in the south it was the northern wall. Worshippers south of the Jordan faced west while those in the west, along the coast, faced east. All the synagogues were thus oriented toward Jerusalem and the Temple Mount, which were the focus of the worshipper's prayer, both physically and spiritually. Fulfilling Psalms 137:6, they set Jerusalem above their greatest joy even when there was no access to the city because of the decrees of its foreign governors.

The entrances to the synagogues in the Land of Israel were therefore located in the wall paralleling the "Jerusalem wall" rather than in the adjacent walls.[41] In the Ezra ha-Sofer synagogue in Egypt, which is of the basilica type, the entrance is on the western side, the wall facing the "Jerusalem wall," but one must remember that this synagogue had been a church that the Jews bought.[42] Indeed, we can see that in this synagogue they built an entrance hall with three entrances from three directions, but the western entrance had a door that was never used, while the entrance doors were on the northern and southern sides of the entrance hall.

We do not know what caused this change in the concept of the entrance, nor can we know whether the entrance hall of Ezra ha-Sofer was not a later addition. However, we must emphasize that in the Spanish synagogues the rule was that the entrance to the synagogue was in a wall next to the "Jerusalem wall" rather than in the wall opposite it. This tradition was continued later in the synagogues in Poland and Germany.[43] However, where in western and eastern Europe the entrance was usually in the middle of the entrance wall, in Spain they placed it close to the western wall, a sizable distance from the "Jerusalem wall" but also in the middle of the longitudinal wall, as in the Cordoba synagogue, the Ibn Shoshan synagogue in Toledo, and the market synagogue in Seville. The first of these is a small synagogue – one can almost say a residential room that was converted into a synagogue – and one cannot analyze it architecturally as a public structure even though many have done so, but in the two other buildings the entrance is not conventional, and the same is true of their entrances (regarding this, see the chapter on the Ibn Shoshan synagogue in Toledo and the market synagogue in Seville). Only in these synagogues, which are presumed to be exceptions, is the entrance in the western wall. However, these synagogues were converted into churches. Thus, even while they were still synagogues, there were needs that required them to build an entrance to one of the side aisles that served as a women's section, which is at least the case in the Toledo synagogue.

One might explain the entrance in the wall adjacent to, but at the further end of, the "Jerusalem wall" in terms of the focus of the ritual in the Sephardic synagogue on the one hand and on the desire not to enter immediately into the prayer hall on the other. The plan was that only after worshippers entered the hall and turned eastward would they be able to see the Holy Ark, whereas if the entrance had been on the wall opposite the "Jerusalem wall," as soon as they opened the door, even entering the building, they would see the Holy Ark, the most sacred structure in the synagogue. Indeed, Rabbi Joseph Caro explained this in that exact way when he set down the laws governing the synagogue.[44]

The entrances to the synagogues were not decorated on the outside, in keeping with the architectural tradition that all the efforts to beautify the premises should be directed to the interior, while almost concealing its exterior. It also accorded with the desire not to emphasize the building from the outside lest it attract unwanted attention that might lead to its being closed. Sometimes they would inscribe a modest blessing in Hebrew on the lintel that read: "This is the gate of the Lord; the righteous will enter through it" (Psalms 118:20) or "Blessed are you in coming and blessed are you in leaving" (Deuteronomy 28:6)[45] but nothing more.

We should note that the entrance was generally not right next to the street, and to enter it one had to enter a courtyard or the synagogue garden, which, too, was protected either by a wall or stone fence of some type. After the worshippers entered the gate, they did not yet enter into the prayer hall but rather the cloakroom, where there was a water basin, the *maskilta*, where they washed their hands. Sometimes there was a staircase that led to the women's section. In large synagogues they built a separate entrance for the women. An entrance in the cloakroom, generally in the wall opposite the entrance from the outside, led into enter the prayer hall. This entrance, too, generally had a door. To leave the building, one used the same system of doors and entrances. Generally, the Spanish synagogues had few entrance doors, and in most cases there was only one. One may assume that that was in order to protect the synagogue. In the synagogues in the Land of Israel in the Mishnaic and Talmudic times, there were in most cases three entrances in the front of the synagogue, which were used for both entrances and exits. It is possible that the reason for this was a desire to preserve the tradition of the entry gates to the Second Temple courtyard.[46]

The doorways to the synagogues in Spain were slightly wider than those to residences but not markedly so, and in no case were they more than two meters (seventy-eight inches) wide. The door itself was made of heavy, thick wood and had two parts. We can tell this because there were two sets of hinges, one on each side of the doorpost. Since the present-day doors are not the original ones, it is difficult to know what decorations or carvings were on them, but one may assume that they were carved according to the finest workmanship of those times, generally with geometric figures and flora. If the outer doors were simple, the inner doors that led into the prayer hall were ornate. The lintel was always straight rather than an arch, which shows us that the doors were simple and massive, meant to offer the synagogue excellent protection against thieves, robbers, and rioters. We can see this from the strong hinges and internal bolts used to lock the synagogues from within. Sometimes there was a small arch above the lintel of the entrance door, but that was only where the entrance was within the inner courtyard.

As opposed to the limited number of entrances and doors, there were numerous windows at the top of the walls, near the roof. A synagogue needs to be illuminated well. The building served as the place where the community gathered for prayer, and in Jewish prayer every person is actively involved and must read the prayer book, unlike Christian prayer in the church, where he congregation is usually passive and the priests conduct the services. The Christian congregation sometimes participates by singing familiar hymns, but worshippers do not pray by themselves. Thus it was possible for the church to remain in semi-darkness, especially as the leaders of the Church wanted to project a mystical and awe-inspiring atmosphere. That was not the case in the synagogue, where they wanted a great deal of light, but preferred that it should be daylight rather than light from oil lamps. Add to that the fact that the synagogue was not meant to be a coercive or awe-inspiring building, and that in many cases the synagogue served as a study hall as well. Such a building requires a great deal of light, and indeed we find in the sources that the Jewish law, as codified by Rabbi Joseph Caro and based on earlier Jewish sources and on the actual practice, especially in Spain, specifies: "One who wishes to build (a building outside the synagogue) opposite the synagogue window may not build it four cubits (six to eight feet) away from the window, but (must build it) further away, because (the synagogue) requires a great deal of light."[47] The *Zohar* adds that "It is proper that the synagogue have twelve windows... and a synagogue without windows is not a proper place in which to pray."[48] As noted earlier, the windows were generally toward the upper part of the wall, but in low buildings and in the small synagogues in the villages, the windows were at the height of a person walking outside, which was a cause for concern. Anyone who passed by could peek inside and see what the Jews were doing. Furthermore, the Church did not want Christians to look inside and see the Jewish ceremonies lest they find them intriguing. As a result, when the windows had to be low, they were generally on the side facing the synagogue courtyard and not on the street side.

The general rule was that the Spanish synagogues had many windows, and the tradition of Rabbi Joseph Caro in his *Shulhan Arukh* was thus nurtured from the architectural reality of these synagogues for hundreds of years before Caro wrote his ruling.

Inside the synagogue halls, the windows were decorated, so that they became an integral part of the decorations of the walls and the interior decoration of the hall space. The window frames were painted in bright colors. The window lintels were usually decorated with horseshoe arches, and small pillars were built or carved in plaster like the window jamb, all in accordance with the finest *mudejar* artistry, which was characteristic of several important Spanish synagogues, especially in Toledo.

In the Samuel ha-Levi Abulafia synagogue in Toledo, we still find that all the windows, which were in every wall, were in the upper part of the building underneath the roof – the illumination floor in our definition. At present, we find that more than half the windows have been plastered over, something referred to in architecture as "a blind window." In other words, in order to have the picture complete they built windows along the entire length of the wall, but a considerable number of them were plastered over so that the hall would be dim rather than bright. It appears to us that originally all these windows were open to allow a maximum of light, and only later, when the synagogue was converted to a church, were the windows plastered over.

One should note that locating the windows high up on the synagogue wall added to the security of the building in terms of theft and also people from outside from looking into it. This, though, presented real on-going problems, such as cleaning the windows and opening and closing them, and to solve these problems they needed a sophisticated and complex system.

The window itself evidently had glass in it that might have been clear or colored, or even vitrage. However, since glass is fragile, we have no original examples of that time, and we are unable to arrive at a definite conclusion about what it was then. In any event, it is worth stressing that there was a problem in Spain in this regard: the winter is bitterly cold, especially in Castile, including snowy and very misty days that require clear glass, but in the summer the sun beats down mercilessly and there is a need for colored glass to filter out the sun's rays. A vitrage window is an intermediate solution to this, for its plaster lattice work only allows for half or even less of the area to transmit light.

In private residences, the windows were protected on the outside with wooden shutters. We have not found any way to clarify whether the synagogue windows had similar protection. This question deserves thought and study.

The Art of Decoration and Embellishment

he task of decorating a Jewish public building used for worship is limited from its inception. The artist does not have the right to express himself freely and to be as creative as his heart and mind might prompt him. As we study the decorations and embellishments in the Spanish synagogues, we will soon see that the community leaders learned how to overcome these obstacles and to adjust the general art to Jewish thought and belief. Even sources that were primarily pagan and had no place in the synagogue infiltrated synagogue art and became basic items in the decoration of religious buildings. The public was able to interpret them as symbols that were in keeping with its faith and beliefs. Already in the first centuries of the Common Era, Talmudic law determined that one may decorate a synagogue with images of animals, but not of human beings.[49] This was a major step forward as opposed to what had been prevalent in Jerusalem during the Second Temple era until its destruction.[50] Behind the concern about the use of human figures was the fear that some members of the congregation, particularly children, might believe that these were images of God, so such images were forbidden.

Dura Europos, fresco in the synagogue hall.

Nevertheless, while the Talmudic prohibition is not a norm but rather a principle that was obligatory for a large number of people, other communities chose to act differently. In the synagogue of Dura-Europos of the first centuries of the Common Era, we find images of human beings in many scenes.[51] Over the generations, it appears that the artists exercised a great deal of freedom and images of human beings were used freely in the synagogues. That was the case in the synagogues at Bet Alfa[52] and at the Tiberias hot springs[53] – the god Helios as the sun, zodiacal signs such as Gemini and Virgo, and the seasons as women with exposed shoulders. In addition, there are complete scenes such as the sacrifice of Isaac in the Bet Alfa synagogue, which show us that the community leaders accepted the general art milieu in their synagogue art even though it diverged from religious law. This was the situation in the Land of Israel and in the lands of dispersion until the Arab conquest in the seventh century C.E.

However, after the Arab conquest, under the influence of Islam and its negative attitude toward images, a change took place in both Christianity and Judaism, and especially among the Jews, regarding the use of images in art.[54] This developed gradually, and in the beginning Islam also followed the Byzantine pattern that was full of images, but gradually the tendency developed not to use images in artistic works, particularly as a result of the pressure of fanatical groups that opposed the rulers. All of this had an effect on Jewish art as well.

The struggle between art as influenced by its environment on the one hand and traditional Jewish conservatism on the other never ceased. In the responsa literature of the Middle Ages and in other written sources of the time, we find various rationales for permitting the use of images and even of full scenes composed of images, and here we refer to art that is used to decorate and embellish synagogues. Sometimes they permitted the use of images on movable sacred objects in the

The Barcelona Haggadah, illustration showing the sacrifice of Isaac.

synagogues, but not on the walls of the synagogues themselves. From the discussions on the subject, it appears that the intention of the communities' financial supporters and leaders was to preserve the faith of their communities. When the community's faith and its general level of observance were high, they would slacken the reins. However, when the community's faith was weak and there was a higher chance of assimilation, we find that the leaders instituted decrees regarding the use of various artistic motifs and limited the freedom of the artists.[55]

In thirteenth- and fourteenth-century Spain, in the synagogues studied in the present review, it appears that the rabbis permitted pictures and decorations on cloth, tapestries, wall hangings, mats, and anything that could be put up and taken down, provided that nothing be drawn permanently on the wall. This detail emerges from the written historical documentation but obviously not from any actual objects, since we are not aware of any decorated walls that still exist today and the hangings did not survive.[56]

One may assume that the hanging decorations such as cloth, mats, and so on, included images and scenes, and we can base our assumption on the artwork found in manuscripts, Biblical scrolls, Passover *Haggadot*, *ketubbot* (marriage contracts), and other miniatures of that era in Spain.[57]

As noted, the Passover *Haggadot*, Biblical scrolls, etc., were decorated by the best of artisans and in abundant colors, as was done even in the most conservative communities in Germany. One may assume that whoever permitted the decoration of the Holy Scriptures and did not feel that this would imperil the faith of his community would not hesitate to permit such decorations in the synagogue hall.

Dyeing fabrics, weaving, and trading with the East were all left in the hands of the Jews. The historical sources note that there were even Jewish artisans who prepared artistic works for the churches.

It is impossible to know the source of the custom to hang decorations but not to paint directly on the walls. Was this done because of pressure

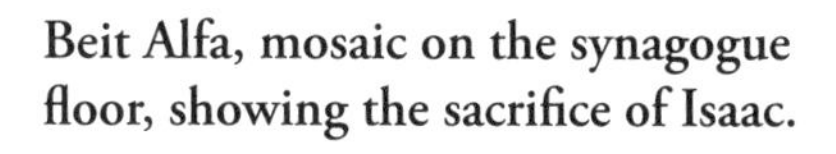

Beit Alfa, mosaic on the synagogue floor, showing the sacrifice of Isaac.

The Barcelona Haggadah, illustration showing the *teivah* for reading the Torah.

from the local authorities or because of an internal Jewish regulation? As noted, we see this rule reflected in the rulings of Rosh, among others.

It is possible that the reason for this has to do with the vicissitudes of the time. During difficult times for the Jews, when the pressure on them increased together with economic and religious decrees, these decorations could be removed and hidden in storehouses until things cooled down. Another possible explanation relates to a more practical consideration: one could switch the decorations in accordance with the seasons and festivals.

Even in those synagogues where we find stucco, we find entire walls with no decoration, which indicates the possibility of using tapestries, mats, and so on as hanging wall decorations. This means that the artistic decorations in the synagogue were of two kinds – permanent and temporary, hangings that could be changed or removed. The permanent artwork was more modest and of a type that could be generally acceptable throughout the generations, whereas the hanging decorations could be bolder, and whenever people tired of them or there was danger to them from hostile mobs, they could be removed and stored away.

Decorative horseshoe arch, emphasizing the artistic ability of the Muslim art in Spain.

There remain only three synagogues in Spain whose artwork is still intact and covers a large area: the small synagogue in Cordoba and the two synagogues in Toledo. We can draw certain general conclusions from them. All three have had undergone preservation work, including a great deal of restoration during the nineteenth and twentieth centuries. This took place after they were declared national sites and were intended for viewing by tourists. It is therefore very difficult to know which of the artwork and decorations are original and which were restored. We should add that when these buildings were used as churches, it was the Church that decorated them. Nevertheless, at first glance it appears to us that the decorations and all of their elements, and especially the inscriptions, are original and were restored properly, in a way that preserved their authenticity as much as possible. One can therefore treat them as Jewish artwork of the thirteenth and fourteenth centuries.

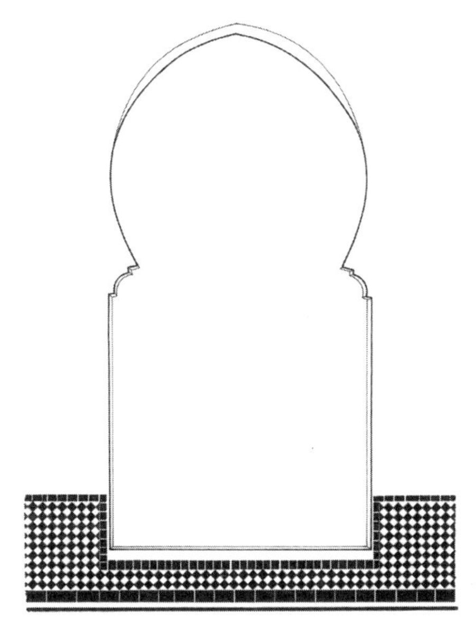

Horseshoe arch, illustrating the delicacy and importance of Muslim art in Spain.

The artwork in general is stucco, using the best Muslim methods under Christian rule – artwork known as Mudejar. It involved various compositions of geometric patterns intertwined with flora, like a divine garden, a paradise on earth. The stucco employs warm and subdued colors. Brown predominates as the background color, and within it one finds a host of colors and sections in green, blue, and even red, in various hues. All of these give the impression of a heavy wall of walnut wood with various carvings highlighted by strong colors.[58]

The geometric and floral stucco panels are enclosed by bands that contain Biblical verses written in square Hebrew script, in most cases in white. The inscriptions are legible, with large letters, even though sometimes they are written from the top to the bottom and not always from right to left, all of this depending on the form of the frame. Thus everyone who came to the synagogue could read them easily. Sometimes one finds an Arabesque within the design. These Arabesques are not Arabic letters but rather a script made to look like a fancy Arabic script, this being an artistic expression in itself. In Hebrew, though, the letters are clear and are not merely "look-alike."

Stucco design, among the finest Islamic art in Spain and north Africa.

The crowns at the top of the pillars in the synagogue hall are sometimes stone, as in the market synagogue in Seville, but in many other cases are made of stucco. It is possible that these latter crowns were originally of stone but were replaced by stucco when the stone wore out. Alternately, that is the way they were originally made. The same is true for the small crowns at the tops of the pillars above the windows in the Samuel ha-Levi Abulafia synagogue in Toledo. The model used for decorating the space in the crowns consisted of broad leaves shaped like a tongue or a sword in the crowns near the windows, or a cone, apples or other succulent fruits such as citrons attached to one another by trailing branches or intertwined ropes, which create unusual crowns on the crowns within the hall pillars.

Mudejar art, which originated among the Muslims, uses a large number of ceramic tiles fired in molds in a variety of colors. These tiles, which are known in Spanish as *azulejos,*[59] were sometimes painted in a single solid color and sometimes they had all types of designs on them, primarily geometric or bright flora. Placing them one next to another created carpets of refreshing color and design. Ceramic tiles were used on the lower parts of the walls and at the bases of the pillars, as can be seen in the Ibn Shoshan synagogue in Toledo. The pillars used ceramic tiles both as a decoration and for protecting the walls when the floors were washed. When used on walls, they served to prevent people from touching the walls. Such tile surfaces can be washed and need little maintenance. In Muslim buildings or Christian buildings built in the Muslim style, we find ceramic tiles covering the entire wall, whereas in the synagogues they are only found at the bottom of the walls. Did they extend up to the height of a person? We could not find an answer to this question, which is one that further research should take up.

Since the Mudejar art in the Spanish synagogues did not deviate from the limits of contemporary art in other buildings, therefore, as an interim conclusion it seems to us that the use of ceramic tiles in the synagogues was in keeping with their use in other buildings, palaces and religious structures of that era in Spain.

The Hebrew Letter as a Basis for Decoration

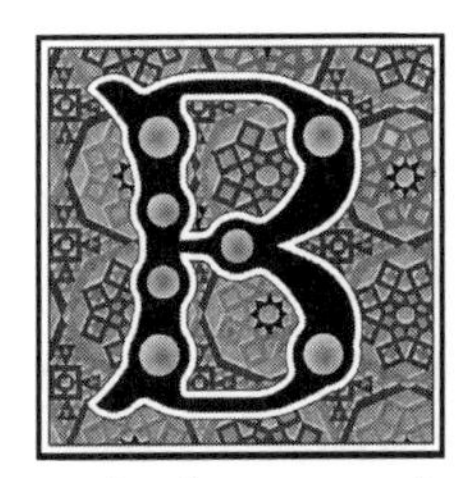

By its nature, the synagogue needs to display various inscriptions. People donated money to build a synagogue or one of its wings so that, among other reasons, the members of their community or group would be aware of their donation. Some wanted to record their own names for posterity, while others wished to records the names of members of their families. This desire led to inscriptions in most of the ancient synagogues in the Land of Israel. These inscriptions were incised into the rock, generally on door lintels and on other architectural sections that stood out. In many cases, the inscriptions, often very long ones, were in the mosaic floors of the synagogues.[60] In one of the synagogues of the Talmudic era in the Land of Israel, a long inscription was found which included the *beraita* of "the borders of the Land of Israel."[61] In the synagogue in Bet Alfa, inscriptions were found explaining the sacrifice of Isaac in accordance with the Biblical verses.[62] In Ein Gedi, at the entrance to the synagogue, there is an inscription cursing anyone who reveals the secrets of the community.[63]

The Spanish synagogues were remarkable in terms of the wealth of engraved inscriptions, including dedications.[64] However, what was unique about Spain was that the use of Hebrew letters in the synagogue architecture was not limited to dedications and, on the contrary, its primary contribution was the introduction of the inscriptions and the Hebrew letters into the decorative and ornamental aspects of

Toledo, the Shmuel HaLevi Abulafia synagogue, examples of decorative letters. The artist used these in decorating the synagogue.

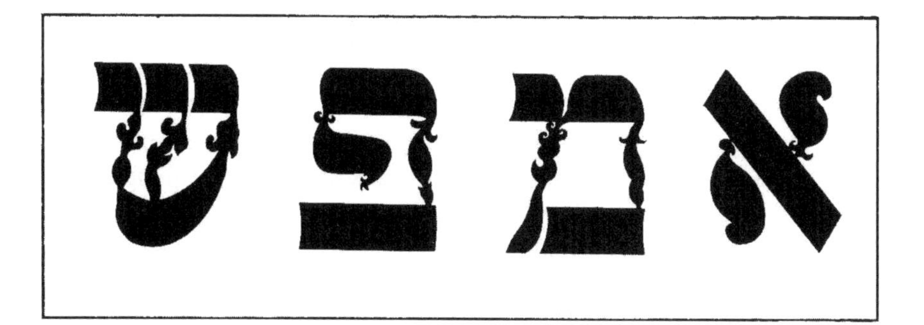

the synagogue. Although this was an almost singular concept in its innovation in the world of synagogue architecture, it was not unique.

Every Jewish visitor who enters a synagogue in Spain, whether it be the Samuel ha-Levi Abulafia synagogue in Toledo or the small synagogue in Cordoba, is moved by the power of the Hebrew inscriptions with which he is confronted. Moshe Ehrenpreis, in his work *Ha-aretz bein mizrah u-ma'arav* (*The Land between East and West*) describes it movingly:

> For the first time, the Hebrew letters were used to decorate a wall.... The Hebrew words of Psalms have survived many persecutions since the Inquisition, and today, as then, [the letters] shine forth in their quiet light; forsaken, neglected, not understood, unheeded, foreign to the environment, they have lived their independent lives for hundreds of years, undefeated, refusing to surrender.[65]

One can understand the emotion felt by a Jew who enters Spain and visits its synagogues and is moved by this evidence of Jewish life, the unequivocal script. But one should not exaggerate the description. It appears that decorations of painted verses had already existed in the Land of Israel at the time of the Talmud, as might well have been the case with the synagogue of Rehov.[66] What little remains there is very difficult to decipher, but there is a hint of the use of the written letter as a decorative element in the synagogue architecture, whether it was used as a means to beautify the synagogue, as a dedication, or whether these were scriptural verses, as we find in the floor mosaics.

The use of Hebrew letters in Spain thus has a basis in ancient traditions, even though there was a great deal of innovation in Spain in terms of the form and the way it was used.[67] The closest and most immediate influence regarding the use of letters is from Muslim architecture, which took Arabic letters and incorporated them into the floral and geometrical stucco sheets in its mosques and palaces. With these letters, where the Muslim artist took a great deal of liberty in incorporating the letters into words, they created fantastic decorated panels. Although the Jewish artists in Spain borrowed the idea, they were limited by the fact that the letters are different and by the way the Hebrew letters are written. Hebrew letters are square and have limited flexibility, as opposed to the rounded Arabic letters, which can create many designs. Therefore the ornate Arabic letter, which in most cases is joined to the letter before or after it, can be incorporated in the geometric and floral design, and this was one of the most accepted themes in this art. The eternal, unending chain, which is expressed by means of quotes that have no beginning or end and that one can begin to read in the middle and has no need to end, reminds the viewer of God, who has no beginning or end.

Incorporating Hebrew letters into decorative art was thus different from incorporating Arabic letters, but was similar it in terms of perception and philosophy. Artists took the letters and used them in bands that created and separated decorative panels, an essential separation between various decorative fields. Instead of appearing monotonous, these bands were instead filled with letters that formed complete quotes. In order to create lines, mosaics used a twisted rope or a double meander, lines winding in and out or crossing one another rectangularly, whereas in Spain they filled the area between the decorative areas with inscriptions in square letters.

When artists found that filling the bands met their needs, they made sure that the passages chosen would consist of significant content. This content was of two kinds: first, laudatory inscriptions and dedications, and second – with greater frequency – entire chapters of the Bible, where the content had a substantive connection to the synagogue and its ritual and as related to the Temple ritual. There was nothing more appropriate for this than the book of Psalms, which includes psalms of praise that mention the Temple and Jewish ritual. Most of the laudatory and dedicatory inscriptions used the same letter design. In several bands a different letter design appears. In the laudatory and dedicatory inscriptions that were located in a conspicuous place and, to a lesser, extent in the separation bands, artists deliberately changed the form of the letter that had been selected for the inscription. Thus there is a difference between the letters in the separation bands and the letters of the dedicatory inscription. This was the case in the Samuel ha-Levi Abulafia synagogue in Toledo and in the small synagogue in Cordoba.

As noted, the verses used in the separation bands were taken from Psalms, sometimes selected verses and at other times entire chapters or parts of chapters. Sometimes the quote was from a *piyyut* or a prayer. Among the verses found in Cordoba, there are the following: "Lord, I have loved the dwelling place of Your house and the place where Your honor dwells" (Psalms 26:8); "I will dwell in Your tabernacle forever; I will trust in the hiding place of Your wings; Selah" (Psalms 61:5). And in another location: "One thing I have desired of the Lord, that I will seek after: that I may dwell in the house of the Lord all the days of my life, to behold the beauty of the Lord and to pray in His temple" (Psalms 27:4). In Toledo: "For the Chief Musician on stringed instruments. A Psalm of David. Hear my cry, O God; attend to my prayer from the end of the earth" (Psalms 61:1–2).[68]

The ideas of the Jewish artists who decorated and adorned the Spanish synagogues generally led them logically to adorn the women's sections with Biblical verses relating to famous Biblical passages dealing with women. Thus, in the small synagogue in Cordoba we find: "I will sing to the Lord, for He has triumphed gloriously" (Exodus 15:1), i.e., the Song of the Sea of Reeds," which Moses and the Children of Israel sang and which Miriam, Moses's sister, led the women in reciting responsively.

We noted earlier that there were verses over the lintels referring to entry, and thus, for example, we find in Toledo: "This is the gate of the Lord into which the righteous shall enter" (Psalms 118:20), or "Blessed are you when you arrive and blessed are you when you depart" (Deuteronomy 28:6), a tradition which stretches back to the decorated synagogue in Alei in Lebanon. This tradition was already widespread in the Talmudic era and at the beginning of the Arab conquest of the Land of Israel, for example in the synagogue in Marut.[69]

The Foci of Synagogue Ritual: The Hekhal, Tevah, Migdal, Amud

The synagogue hall was furnished in accordance with the community's liturgical and ritual needs. Jewish ritual and prayer dictated how the artists set up the interior of the building. Two main foci, the *hekhal* and the *tevah,* were needed for the synagogue ritual, along with two secondary ones. These were the terms used by Spanish Jewry at the time, and are used to this day by those Jewish communities that are derived from it.

Among Ashkenazic Jewry, even though these two were the main foci of the synagogue, the terms used for them were different. The *hekhal* (literally, "the Temple") was known as the *aron ha-kodesh* (literally, "the Holy Ark"), whereas the *tevah* (literally, "the pulpit") was known as the *bimah* (literally, "the platform"). The differences in names also reflect the differences in these appurtenances in the synagogue. In Ashkenazic synagogues, the place where the Torah scrolls are kept is a modest structure, like a closet, whereas in the Sephardic synagogue the Torah scrolls are in a room, hence the term *hekhal.* The same was true for the *tevah*, the place where the Torah scroll is read. At the beginning

Portable *heikhal* made of wood. In the top half the Torah scrolls were stored, whereas in the bottom half *shofarot* and other important sacred objects were kept. This was a simple piece of furniture into which a great deal of effort was expended in decorating the top.

of the Spanish era it was a wooden table and possibly even a movable one, as had been the case in the synagogues in the Land of Israel during Talmudic times, and hence it was known as the *tevah*, meaning "the Box." In the Ashkenazic synagogue, the platform where the Torah scroll was read became a prime appurtenance of the synagogue and therefore a great deal was invested in it until it became the center of the synagogue. Hence its name: *bimah*, "the platform."

Along with these two primary components of the Sephardic synagogue, there were two others, the *migdal* (literally, "the tower") and the *amud* – the lectern. In the Ashkenazic synagogue these would be known as the *duchan* and the *amud*, but they were not significant. Many synagogues did not have a *migdal*, and the *amud*, where the cantor stood during the prayers, never developed into an independent component of the synagogue.[70]

In studying the synagogues in Spain, a question arises: where were the synagogue foci, especially the *tevah* (the Ashenazic *bimah*)? The location of the *hekhal* (the *aron kodesh*) is clear, for there are remnants of them in ancient ruins and a clear tradition of their placement: they are always on the eastern wall of the structure. In this regard, "east" means a general alignment toward Jerusalem, for the synagogues in the Land of Israel during Mishnaic and Talmudic times faced Jerusalem. In the Galilee, it was the wall that faced Jerusalem and in the rest of the country it was the *hekhal* that they faced during prayer. There is no finer or more appropriate place than the wall that faces Jerusalem as the place for the *hekhal* or *aron*. In Europe it was always in that general direction, i.e., the east.

We have no details as to what the *hekhal* looked like. The Spanish synagogues which survived were converted to churches, and it was in that form that they came down to us. The focus of Christian ritual is also the east, so that when the Christians converted the synagogues into churches they reorganized the eastern wall for their own needs and tastes and therefore destroyed the original *hekhalot* to the extent that we are unable to know their precise original form and structure. But we can use drawings and information, as well as the tradition of the Spanish synagogues as it was transmitted by the exiles to Italy, North Africa, Turkey, and even to the Land of Israel. Although this does not offer a definite answer to the question, nevertheless one can begin an investigation of the historical truth with sure steps.

In the synagogues in the Land of Israel in the Talmudic era, in most cases the *hekhal* was a larger structure than the *aron kodesh* to which we are accustomed. At least it enjoyed a permanent structure of its own – namely the niche in the wall facing Jerusalem.71 As opposed to this, in the synagogues outside the Land of Israel from the Middle Ages onward, no *aron* has been found that was an independent structure within the synagogue. At least we are sure that there was no large niche – an apse which would extend outside the building line on the eastern wall. In general, the *aron* was a wooden structure next to the eastern wall or that was inserted into the wall like a wall closet. As noted, this is reflected in the change in the name from *hekhal* ("temple") to *aron* ("closet"). The *aron* also served as a reminder of the *aron* in the First Temple, which was a wooden closet in which the Two Tablets were kept, where their equivalent in the synagogue ritual is taken by the Torah scrolls.[72]

The architecture of the synagogues in Spain shows us that the *hekhal* was a small room, but separate from the synagogue main hall. The room, which stood independently, was where the Torah scrolls were placed for safe-keeping. This room had its own doors, in front of which was a *parokhet* a curtain. The wooden doors were carved artistically in the finest fashion. As noted, the name used for the room, *hekhal*, testifies to its construction and structure.

In many synagogues in Europe and in the east, from the Middle Ages on, the builders intensified the focus on the *aron* by having steps lead upward to it. The *aron* was built on a higher level than the synagogue, at least to the height of the *bimah*, so that the Torah scrolls would not be stored at a lower level than that occupied by people in the synagogue, even if the only people who might be higher would be those reading from the Torah scrolls on the *bimah* As far as the

Elaborate *heikhal* in the Jerusalem wall of the synagogue. In front of it is a raised platform, used only for the *heikhal*.

Spanish synagogues are concerned, we are unable to ascertain how high the *hekhal* stood. The cupboards that exist today are at the same level as the synagogue floor. It is possible that the *tevah*, which was a wooden table, stood on the floor and was not on a higher level. However, there is the possibility that in order to open the *aron* in the *hekhal* one had to climb several steps, except that all evidence of this was destroyed when the buildings were converted to churches. In Italian synagogues the *tevah* and *aron* were usually raised.

As noted, we cannot be certain of the structure of the *aron* within the *hekhal* in all the Spanish synagogues. In the synagogue in Cordoba, which is small and not even a public building, the *hekhal* is a very large structure relative to the size of the synagogue hall. The *hekhal* of this synagogue does not extend out into the street, and it is contained completely within the width of the eastern wall of the synagogue. As noted above, one cannot argue about the walls of the *aron* in the Spanish synagogues but can only surmise based on *aronot kodesh* in Italy, whose architecture is close to the architectural tradition of Spain. Similarly, one can thus only surmise as to what the doors of the *aron* in Spain were like.[73]

This is all the more true regarding the nature and design of the *parokhet* – the curtain – in front of the *hekhal*. At the same time, we do know that the Jewish community invested a great deal in designing and creating these curtains. For this, they chose expensive cloth that they embroidered with gold and silver threads. The idea of the *parokhet* was taken from the design of the Temple and the Holy of Holies within it, where the non-rigid *parokhet* served as a partition between the holy and profane – a partition that existed and was tangible on the one hand, and was ethereal and non-existent on the other. The *parokhet* was of special importance in the design of the synagogue hall where the hall was used for study and other events that might be of a secular

The *heikhal*, i.e., the *aron kodesh*, in whose design a great deal of effort was invested. In front of the *heikhal* was a *parokhet* - a curtain – symbolizing the *parokhet* which separated the Holy of Holies in the Temple in Jerusalem.

nature. In such cases, a partition between the holy, as represented by the *hekhal* and the *aron hakodesh*, and the hall itself was essential. In any event, the beauty and magnificence of the *parokhet* enabled the synagogue elders to boast about their first-rate treasure.

The other focus of the synagogue, the *tevah* upon which the Torah scroll was placed to be read to the community – was a significant focal point in the synagogue liturgy, and it had its own distinct design, for its status demanded this.

Its name indicates first and foremost that it was a modest item, a type of movable table. Regarding the architecture of the ancient synagogues in the Land of Israel, and especially in the Galilee, there were those who thought that the *tevah* was a movable box on wheels.[74] Over time, this movable table was transformed into a permanent structure in the synagogue. When the simple table was transformed into permanent furniture, it nevertheless retained a certain temporary element since it was made of wood. Even though the builders added a canopy and decorations to it, the fact that it was made of wood still implied a certain temporariness, and thus it was of somewhat lesser importance than the *hekhal*. Over time it became a solid structure built of stone and clay, and its name was changed from *tevah* to *bimah*, primarily in the Ashkenazic congregations.[75]

Originally, the *teivah* was a simple wooden table with a decorated cloth on top of it.

In those places where the *tevah* was built of stone and became an integral part of the structure, we can find its location in the buildings, as remnants of them have survived. The same is true in those places where they were massive wooden structures, for they still exist and one can find their position and the way they were used.[76] That was not the case in Spain, because of all the synagogues in this country no relics of the *tevot* have survived. Thus we can only hypothesize where they were located. We can do this to a certain extent by examining the other foundations of the synagogue building, such as the locations of the entry doorway and of the women's section.

In many synagogues and throughout history, the *tevah* was located either in the middle of the prayer hall or close to its rear wall of the prayer hall – that is, close to the western wall in the European countries, as stated by Joseph Caro in the *Shulhan Arukh*, which states: "The *bimah* is built in the middle of the synagogue where the one reading the Torah will stand, so that everyone can hear him...."[77] This law also states that the entrance to the synagogue must in the wall opposite the one where the *hekhal* is located – that is, opposite the wall where the *aron kodesh* is located. In the European countries, including Spain, the entrance is in the western wall.

The *teivah* was built with great attention to detail, and with a canopy above. It is raised from the floor level, and one must climb steps to ascend to it.

This law was made after the expulsion from Spain, and although it can be claimed that the laws of the *Shulhan Arukh* reflect the traditions of synagogue construction in Spain, it would appear that there were various traditions. While some regard the architecture of

The *teivah* was improved upon and became ever more ornate. Here this one has two sets of steps, one for ascending and one for descending, symbolizing the different entrances to the Temple Mount.

the synagogues in Italy as reflecting the tradition of the architecture of the Spanish synagogues, in the Sephardic Italian synagogues the *tevah* or *bimah* is close to the wall opposite the *hekhal* wall – that is, close to the western wall.[78] One can understand the intention of the planner who placed the foci of the synagogue as the extreme foci: the *hekhal* by the eastern wall and the *tevah* by the western wall. According to this tradition, the Torah is read before the entire congregation, whereas if the *tevah* is in the center of the prayer hall, half the congregation is behind it. Thus it would appear that that was the main reason for moving the *tevah* from the center to the western wall. However, there was a catch to this, for where the prayer hall was large and the distance between the front and the back considerable, those who sat along

The plan of a synagogue with four central columns dictates that the *teivah* is in the center of the synagogue.

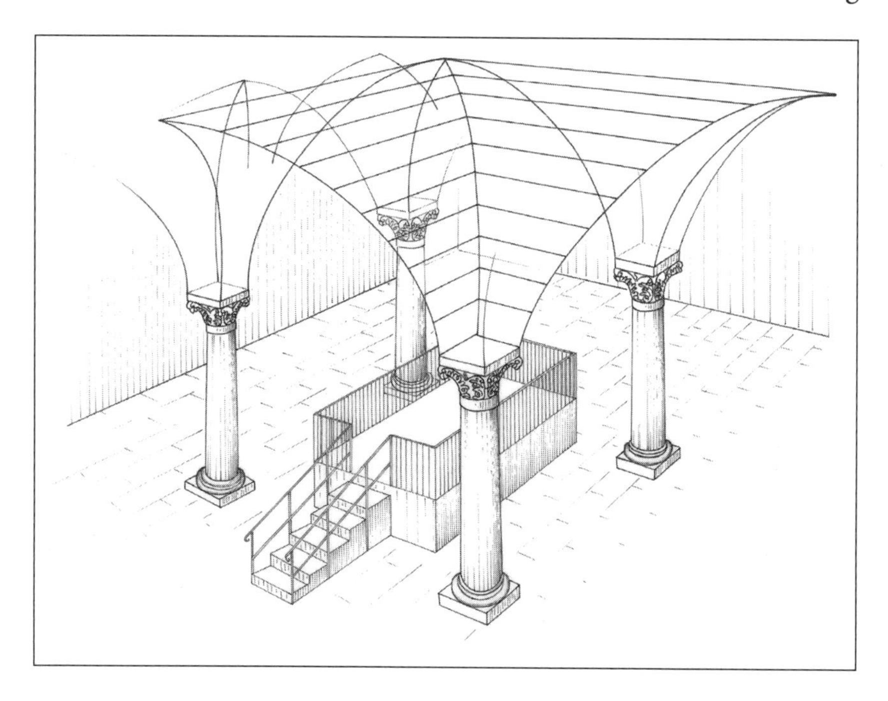

the eastern wall – and these were the most important officials in the synagogue – might find it hard to hear. Furthermore, one can say that where the *tevah* is in the middle hall, the reading of the Torah, which is one of the most important elements of the synagogue ritual, is considered central to the service.

The original furniture did not remain in the Spanish synagogues, and even where items such as the *tevah* had been constructed of solid material, these were dismantled and removed when the synagogues were converted into churches. As the entrances are in the northern or southern wall and not in the western wall, one might possibly conclude that the *tevah* was not in the center but was built close to the western wall. If that was indeed the case, it was impossible to construct the entrance where it should have been. This was the case, for example, in the Samuel ha-Levi Abulafia synagogue in Toledo, in the synagogue in the old district in Segovia, and in others. But in the Ibn Shoshan synagogue in Toledo and in the market synagogue in Seville, the entrances were both in the long wall – the northern or southern wall – but there were also entrances in the western wall opposite the *hekhal*. It is possible that these entrances on the western wall were added at a later time, after the synagogues were transformed into churches. In Toledo, if the door in the western wall is an original one, one should regard this as the entry room to the women's section.

The Barcelona *Haggadah*, with a drawing of the preacher's stand.

As far as the small synagogue in Cordoba is concerned, one may assume with a greater degree of certainty that the *tevah* was near the western wall. This assertion is based on a small niche in the western wall. It is clear, though, that that niche was too small for the construction of the *tevah*, and it might have been for the place where the reader stood. It is more logical to assume that this niche is a remnant of a wall closet which was meant to keep prayer books or other items and that it does not indicate one of the synagogue foci. In any event, the small synagogue in Cordoba cannot be evaluated in terms of the standard criteria of architecture, for we are referring here to a small room of about six by six meters (less than twenty by twenty feet), whose internal structure is irrelevant in terms of the location of the *tevah* One should note, though, that most scholars regard this structure as typical of the Spanish synagogues.[79]

Reconstruction of the preacher's stand in the synagogue hall, based on the drawing in *Haggadot.*

It would appear that their error was derived from the fact that the analyses were based solely on the information they received about this building and not from seeing it or having any real acquaintance with the structure itself. In our opinion, the *tevah* in this synagogue could have been in the center of the room or close to the western wall. In either case it would have served the ritual needs of the congregation very well.

The *bimah* or *tevah* was generally on a higher level than the floor of the synagogue hall. It was between half a meter to a meter (19.5 to 39

The "Bird *Haggadah,"* with the cantor praying before the *amud.* In order not to use a human image, they substituted birds' heads.

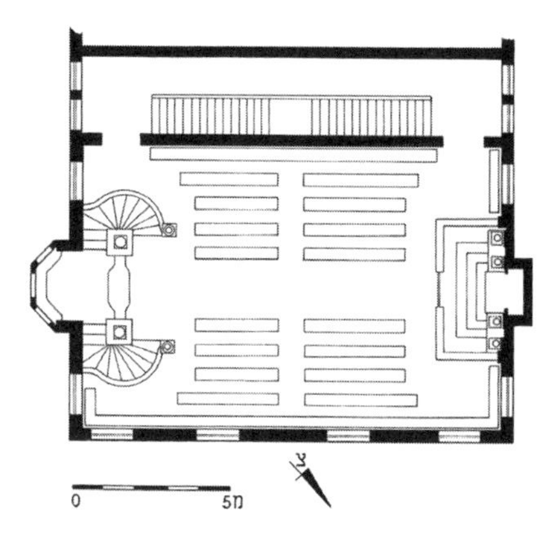

The plan of the Oriental synagogue, Livantino, in Venice, according to Finkerfeld, in 1568. The *heikhal* is in the east, to the right, and the *teivah* is in the west, to the left. In the south is the entrance hall and the steps to the women's section. In many Italian synagogues, the *teivah* was located on the wall opposite the *heikhal,* and not in the middle of the hall. Generally, these were not large halls. Is that derived from the Spanish tradition?

inches) higher than the floor, so that those who read from the Torah could be seen and their voices could be heard and echo throughout the hall. This was a way to increase respect for the Torah.

Originally, the *tevah* was made simply of wood, and the first ones may even have been on wheels in order to make them mobile. The *tevah* could then be rolled into a side room, freeing the hall for various uses such as communal meetings or study when it was not being used for prayer. Later, when the view that the synagogue should be used only for its primary purpose became predominant, there was no reason not to make the *tevah* into a permanent structure. It was then that builders began to construct at least the base of the *tevah* as a solid structure using rocks, bricks, and clay. There were cases where the base, too, was built of massive wood and its columns anchored permanently to the floor. In both cases, the *tevah* above the base was built of wood or steel and included lattice work, railings, and pergolas that extended above the heads of those reading the Torah, like a decorated wedding canopy. This massive construction made it into the focus of the *hekhal* and the most elaborate focus of the synagogue. One can see this in the Italian synagogues and those of the Land of Israel during the Ottoman period, or in some synagogues in Poland or Germany.[80]

In the dedication inscription in the Samuel ha-Levi Abulafia synagogue in Toledo, we find that among the other items mentioned as having been dedicated in the synagogue, there is reference to "a wooden *migdal* (tower) for religious reading."[81] Is this a reference to the *tevah,* or was this another object in the synagogue hall? We believe that it was another object. Had the one who dedicated it wanted to refer to the *tevah,* he would have used a word that everybody knew. Also, had he been referring to the *tevah,* the text would have stated that the purpose was "for Torah reading" and not "for religious reading." Thus, this must be a different object.

Along with the *hekhal* and the *tevah,* which were the main foci of the synagogue, two other essential elements, the *migdal* and the *amud,* were part of it. Although the *migdal* was usually built of wood, its foundation was built of stone or brick. In most cases, it was located in the southern side of the synagogue, close to the wall or next to it. If the synagogue was shaped like a basilica, divided into three or more sections, the *migdal* was attached to one of the pillars of the middle hall. It was generally attached to the pillar closest to the *hekhal,* the eastern wall, but we have also found cases where it was in the middle of the long hall or in the northern row of pillars of the central hall. The *migdal* appears several times in the miniatures that decorate the Holy Scriptures or in Passover *Haggadot.* In most cases it was described as the *tevah* of the synagogue, but that is not correct since it is a separate element with its own purpose.[82] It would appear that it was to this object that Samuel ha-Levi, who offered the dedication, was referring when he wrote: "A wooden *migdal* for religious reading."[83]

We also find in the churches in the Land of Israel during the Byzantine era that a wooden stand was set up for the liturgical needs of the Christian ritual. The architectural term for that structure was *ambo,*[84] the modern word "pulpit" being an appropriate translation, and in the Middle Ages it was referred to as "a wooden *migdal* for religious reading." Like this, it appears that similar wooden platforms were constructed in the ancient synagogues in the Land of Israel. It would appear that both the Jewish and Christian religious buildings were copied from the Muslim mosque. In the Muslim mosque

Khorazin, "Moses' Katedra" from a synagogue. It is made of basalt rock. It was evidently a seat of honor for one of the community heads.

architecture, there is always, on the western side of the *mihrab* and close to it a pulpit known as the *mimbar* or *minbar.*[85]

In the Spanish synagogues this object, the *dukhan* or the "wooden *migdal* for religious reading," was of great importance in the synagogue milieu and the other public events that took place there in addition to religious services. Community leaders used it in order to address the people about important communal issues. It was also used by emissaries from other countries or cities who collected money for aid of one type or another, and was also used to announce new decrees or inform the community of pogroms against their co-religionists. Sometimes a visiting dignitary used it as a platform for a speech or Torah lecture. One may assume that if a non-Jew was invited to address the community, he would speak from the *migdal.* Here we are not talking about a curious non-Jew or a private guest, but emissaries of the king or the government. For example, in the great debate held in the Barcelona synagogue between Nahmanides and Christian delegates in the king's presence, the debaters used that pulpit because it was a "neutral corner," as it were, that did not have the sanctity of the *tevah*, which was used for reading the Torah scroll.[86] A "*migdal* for religious reading" would be most appropriate for reading the government's announcements to the Jews, especially as such a pulpit appears time and again in Spanish miniatures.

The fourth element in the religious structure of the synagogue is the *amud,* a platform or simple wooden table upon which the cantor would place his prayer book and that enabled him to run the service properly. At first the *amud* was a movable object, nothing more than a stable wooden stand upon which a piece of wood was fixed to hold the prayer book, like the type of stand used by musicians to hold their music. Later, the *amud* became a permanent, immovable fixture in the synagogue. It was usually located to the right of the *hekhal* and next to the eastern wall, while in other cases it was in front of the *hekhal.* In front of it was a sign in Hebrew that read: "I have set the Lord always before me" (Psalms 16:8). We have no conclusive proof that this existed in the Spanish synagogues, but it is present in various miniatures such as in the "Bird Haggadah," and the cantor stands in front of it. Rabbi Joseph Caro, author of the *Shulhan Arukh*, notes the existence of the *amud* and even specifies its place, stating: "When the cantor prays, his face is toward the Holy [Ark],"[87] meaning toward the *hekhal* and the eastern wall. In this case, the cantor stands with his back to the congregation. Unlike the *tevah* and the *hekhal*, the *amud* is of secondary importance, and this was also expressed in the resources invested in building it, as with the "*migdal* for religious reading," the pulpit.

Another element in the functioning of the synagogue was the congregation and the way its seating was arranged. Here, too, we have no first-hand information, not in regard to how the benches looked and not how they were arranged in the prayer hall. Ashtor, when discussing the synagogues in Muslim Spain, speaks of people sitting on mats upon the ground, as is the custom among Muslims in their mosques.[88] There is no doubt that Ashtor's descriptions stem from the customs of the Muslim mosque. According to him, it was logical that the when the Jew prayed he would imitate his Muslim neighbor, but there is no proof of this. One should note that the Jewish prayer service is very different from the Muslim one in content and ritual, and there is no reason to assume that the Jews sitting on the floor would have taken this idea from Muslim practice. It is clear that the churches in Spain were not influenced by the Muslim world in its seating arrangements or order of the prayers. Any influence was expressed in art and forms, but not in the way the ritual was conducted.

In the *Shulhan Arukh* we find instructions regarding the seating arrangements in the synagogue. They show that the worshippers sat on chairs, and how the chairs were arranged. Here we are referring to an era a little later than the expulsion of the Jews from Spain and from their synagogues, which took place toward the end of the fifteenth century. He writes: "The elders sit with the faces toward the people while all the rest of the people sit in rows, facing toward the Ark and toward the elders."[89] From these descriptions we see that there were rows of seats paralleling the width of the synagogue, with the worshippers' backs to the west. In the front, on both sides of the *hekhal* along the eastern wall sat the community leaders, with their backs to Jerusalem and their faces toward the congregation. From the seating arrangements in ancient synagogues and in various later traditions it appears that there were no fixed seating patterns, except that the leadership sat with their backs to the eastern wall while they faced the west. Sometimes the seats were parallel to the eastern and western walls, but in other synagogues they ran parallel to the northern and southern walls with two and three rows on either side, and the row closest to the northern and southern walls somewhat raised. This created a large empty space in the middle of the synagogue that enabled them to place chairs in rows parallel to the eastern and western walls. Here, the rows running the length of the synagogue were fixed, while the chairs placed in the center section could be moved, so that the hall could be used for other purposes. In the ancient synagogues, even those of the Temple era, we find rows of stone benches around the four walls, where the center of the hall remained empty.[90]

In the Ezra ha-Sofer synagogue in Fostat, Egypt, the chairs are movable, and they are arranged in lengthwise rows along the northern and southern walls and beneath the women's section in the side sections of the synagogue. It is true that that is the seating arrangement at present, but it is quite possible that this arrangement simply copies the

"Elijah's chair," beautifully decorated, from a synagogue in Italy.

Toledo, the Shmuel HaLevi Abulafia synagogue, canopy next to the entrance for the notables.

one used throughout the years. In our view, in Spain the community leaders would sit with their backs to the eastern wall, facing the congregation. In the middle hall the congregation sat in rows, facing the leaders toward the east, whereas in the side sections there were rows running the length of the hall. This arrangement allowed the community members maximum participation in the rituals.

There were two more semi-architectural objects in the synagogue. Although they are known by two different names, they may have had a single function. These go back in antiquity to the very beginnings of the synagogue or at least from the time of the Mishnah and the Talmud. One was known as Cathedra de Moshe,[91] while the second one was known as Elijah's Chair.[92] These are lavish chairs made of stone or wood upon which pillows and silk cloths were placed. We cannot know whether the two names represent the same function. Elijah's Chair has traditionally been used in synagogues as the chair upon which the *sandak* (the godfather) sits while holding the infant boy during the circumcision ceremony. It is possible that this was the same function performed with the stone Cathedra de Moshe. Another possibility is that this elaborate stone chair was used by the person expounding on Jewish law or giving a homiletic discourse. Whatever the function of these chairs might have been, a tremendous amount of artistic effort was involved in constructing them, which shows that they must have been of great importance in the synagogue ritual. One may assume that these were also to be found in the Spanish synagogues, even though we have absolutely no physical evidence of them.

There was one other item in the Spanish synagogues that was not common even in Spain. We find it only in only one case. This refers to an exquisite structure with a type of canopy, attached to the southern wall of the synagogue, close to the eastern wall and by the women's section. As noted, it was only found in one synagogue in Spain, in the Samuel ha-Levi Abulafia synagogue in Toledo. On the southern wall there is an entrance to a small, exquisite room, and to its west and attached to it is a most beautiful decorated canopy. These indicate an unusual function.[93] One might hypothesize that this was not part of the original synagogue but rather was added during the time that it was a church. However, there is no proof of this. On the contrary, during the Spanish regime, with the aid of architects who are familiar with the site and historians who renovated and restored the synagogue to the way it had been, they left this added room without explaining why, for they were of the opinion that this was part of the original synagogue. Our view is that this facility, both the room and the canopy that served the ornate room inside it, was for the use of Samuel ha-Levi Abulafia, a minister of the king, when he came to the synagogue. It was like the *maqsura* room in a mosque,[94] a private, well-protected chamber for the caliph or king when he came to pray. There was a similar proviso in churches. As we know the lifestyle of Samuel ha-Levi Abulafia, how he lorded it over the people, how he indulged in royal trappings as seen in the dedicatory inscriptions in the synagogue,[95] it is certainly likely that ha-Levi, who was far from humble or modest, built himself a private chamber in the synagogue that he built at his own expense.

Was a canopy something in other synagogues that served the high Jewish government officials and community leaders in Spain? We have no information. It is possible that a historical study or a study of the poetry and prose of Spanish Jewry will be able to add information in this regard particular structure in Toledo.

Summary

undreds of synagogues were built in Spain for its various Jewish communities. The first of these were built during the first centuries of the Common Era under pagan Roman rule and afterwards under Christian Roman rule, under barbaric Christian kings – the Visigoths – and thereafter under Muslim rule, which in most cases was tolerant toward Jews and

Judaism, and finally under the Christian Spanish kings who took the land back from the Muslims. For fifteen hundred years Jewish communities were spread throughout the country, and Jewish culture flourished and attained heights which had never been reached until their time. Spanish Jewry nourished and strengthened Jews throughout their dispersion, both in spirit and in content. The communal building of these communities was the synagogue, together with the auxiliary service buildings linked to it – the *mikveh*, the study hall, and so on. Of all these hundreds of buildings, a mere few survive, as if plucked from the fire. Many of the rest suffered wanton destruction, others were converted to churches, and in other cases to granaries or village public buildings used by all the local Spanish villagers.

While the study of these synagogues began in the nineteenth century and received a great deal of impetus during the mid-twentieth century by scholars such as Francisco Cantera-Burgos, we are still at the very beginning of this topic. There are still many synagogue ruins in Spain, and a great deal of information has not yet become available in written sources such as prose, poetry, and various documents. The study of synagogues in the Iberian peninsula is still in its infancy, and the present work is but a small step up the ladder.

The window decoration in the Shmuel HaLevi Abulafia synagogue in Toledo.

Chapter 4 The Shmuel ha-Levi Abulafia Synagogue in Toledo

ne of the most impressive synagogues among those that survived in Spain is the synagogue on the western edge of the Jewish Quarter in Toledo. It was built by order of Don Shmuel ha-Levi Abulafia, who financed its construction, and remains standing to this day.

A new king, Don Pedro, later Pedro III (the Cruel), ascended the Spanish throne in the second half of the fourteenth century. As was customary in the Christian royal courts of the time, Jews known for their great talents and abilities served in high positions in Don Pedro's court. Don Shmuel ha-Levi Abulafia, the builder of this synagogue, was the highest-placed official in King Pedro's court. He was one of the pillars of the Jewish community in Toledo, one of the most prominent Jewish communities in Spain at that time, and even served as the community

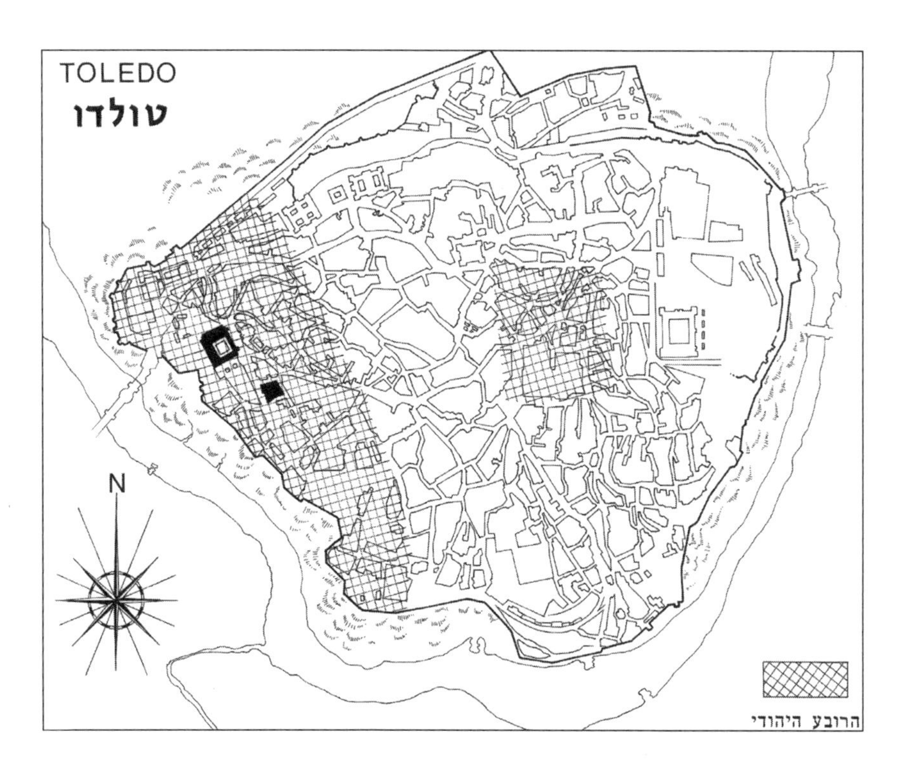

Toledo, map of the city and the Jewish Quarters.

leader, the equivalent of its president. His position in the court was that of minister of the treasury, and he was even given the title of Tesorero Mayor del Rey, Royal High Treasurer. Although he eventually lost the king's favor, during the first years of Don Pedro's reign he was a mainstay in the royal court. In addition to his position as minister of finance he also acted as the foreign minister, serving as a mediator and formulating government policy.[1]

Toledo, home of Shmuel HaLevi Abulafia, which later became the home of El Greco.

The Abulafia family, whose members lived in Toledo and in Seville, is well known in historical sources. Remnants of tombstone inscriptions of the family were discovered in the old cemeteries in Toledo. The first names Shmuel, Meir, and Levi are repeated over the course of generations of this family. These all attest to the exalted positions of the family members in the community and in the royal court. The Abulafias were not known for their great modesty.[2]

The synagogue built by Don Shmuel ha-Levi, the royal finance minister, was planned by the Jewish architect Meir Abdali[3] who, it appears, was also a member of the Abulafia family. In the dedication plaque in the synagogue, the initiator and builder of the synagogue is listed as Rabbi Meir: "We erected this building with the aid of our sages and the great graces of God were with us, for the wise master Rabbi Meir, of blessed memory, enlightened us."[4]

The synagogue was built close to Don Shmuel ha-Levi's home. It served his family and the Jews living in the area, which one may surmise were members of the extended Abulafia family.

About two hundred years later, a number of decades after the expulsion of the Jews from Spain, the building was given to the famed Greek painter El Greco. Nowadays the building is a museum describing how it was set up and used at the time of El Greco. In principle, it also preserves the way it was used as a residence by Don Shmuel ha-Levi.[5]

The year in which the construction of the synagogue and its wings was completed was 1355. As was customary in that era and in general regarding the dating of Jewish communal buildings, the builders alluded to the year by means of a quote – by using the *gematria* values of certain letters of the verse, which were emphasized. In this synagogue as well, which had numerous inscriptions, the builders used a sentence to denote the year of the completion:[6] "The day on which the building was completed was great and good for the Jews." The Hebrew letters for "good for the Jews" were emphasized, as their *gematria* value totaled 117. We can therefore assume that the building was completed in the Hebrew year 5117 (in most cases, the thousands are ignored in these figures) –that is, in 1356–1357.

Toledo, Church of St. John of the Catholic royalty, a decorated aisle in the cloister.

After the Jews were expelled from Spain, the building and its wings were transferred to the Order of the Knights of Calatrava, who used the main hall of the synagogue as a burial ground for the leaders of the Order.[7] The Knights eventually transferred the building to the Jesuits,

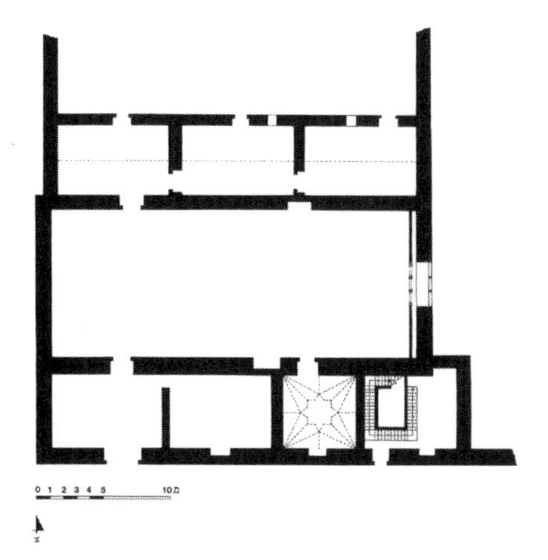

Toledo, Shmuel HaLevi Abulafia synagogue, plan of the ground level.

who converted the hall, which faces east, into a church under a new name, El Transito de Nuestra Señora.[8] The Jesuits also adapted the building to the needs of Christian ritual and customary church services.[9]

In the nineteenth century, the Spanish government announced that El Transito was no longer a church, and the building was declared a national heritage site that preserved the contribution of the Jews to Spain. Accordingly, it was converted to a museum of Toledo and Spanish Jewry. Since the building had changed hands so many times between the expulsion of the Jews and the nineteenth century it suffered considerable damage, but its basic plan was unaffected and many of its original Hebrew inscriptions, which had been covered over, still remained. Once the building was declared a national heritage site, it was renovated as a synagogue. The plaster was peeled off, revealing many inscriptions. However, the damage it had suffered over the years makes it impossible to glean all the information and the data which we would have liked to derive from this rare building.

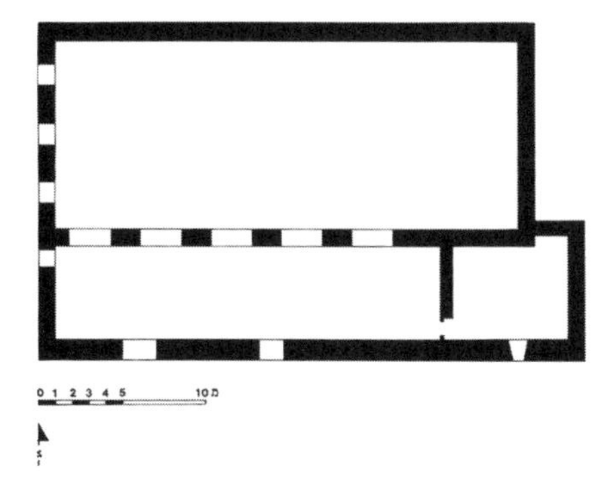

Toledo, Shmuel HaLevi Abulafia synagogue, plan of the women's section.

Architectural Description

he first architectural analysis of the synagogue building plans was that of Otto Czekelius, who even published them.[10] Francisco Cantera-Burgos conducted an important study about the Jewish synagogues in Spain, which he published in Spanish.[11] His study deals primarily with the many inscriptions which were revealed in this synagogue. In his architectural analysis, he accepts the proposals of his predecessor, Czekelius.

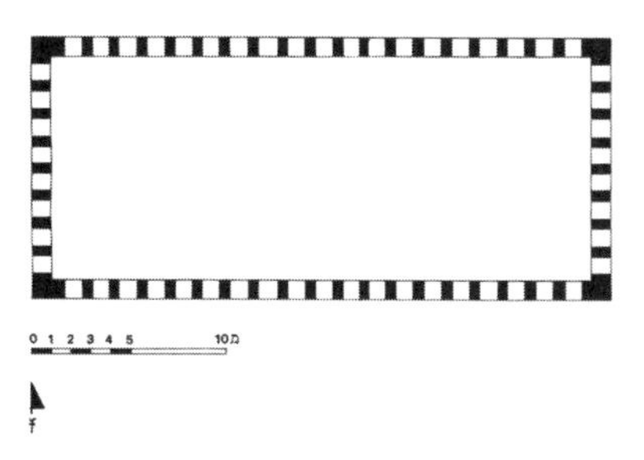

Toledo, Shmuel HaLevi Abulafia synagogue, plan of the illumination level.

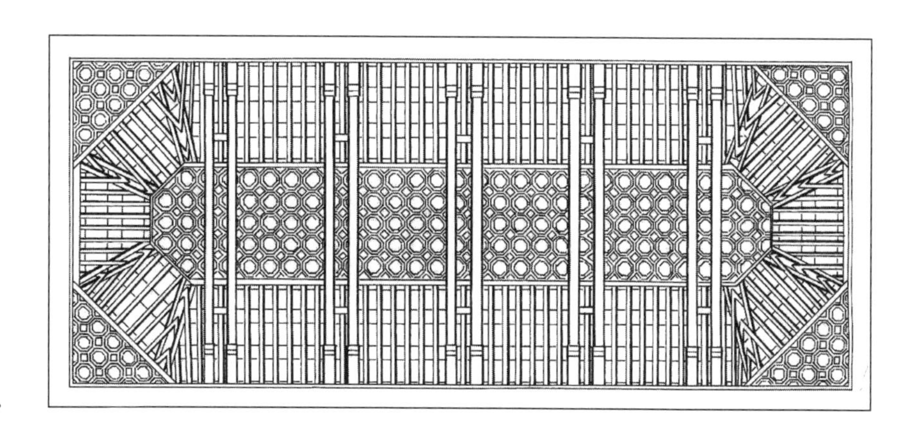

▶ Toledo, Shmuel HaLevi Abulafia synagogue, plan of the wooden ceiling.

The Architectural Plans: the Ground Floor, the Main Hall and the Wings

he synagogue was built using a plan of a single long central hall. One who studies the plan can see that it is based on a basilica – a central hall and two side halls, one on either side of the main hall, underneath a single roof. Indeed, in this building, too, this plan is there, but it is not like the customary basilica. Generally, in basilica plans the main hall and side halls make up a single large hall, with columns of pillars creating a separation between the main hall and the side halls. These pillars are necessary for the roofing of the wide spaces. However, in this case the side halls are totally separate wings off the main hall, separated from it by massive walls. Since there are doors between the wings and the central hall, the building cannot be regarded as a classical basilica, as many churches and synagogues are, even though in the plan itself the proportions and form remain those of a basilica.[12] Further research could prove that a more ancient synagogue, built according to the plan of a classical basilica, preceded the present building on this spot.

Toledo, Shmuel HaLevi Abulafia synagogue, cross-section of the breadth of the synagogue and the view toward the *heikhal* wall in the east.

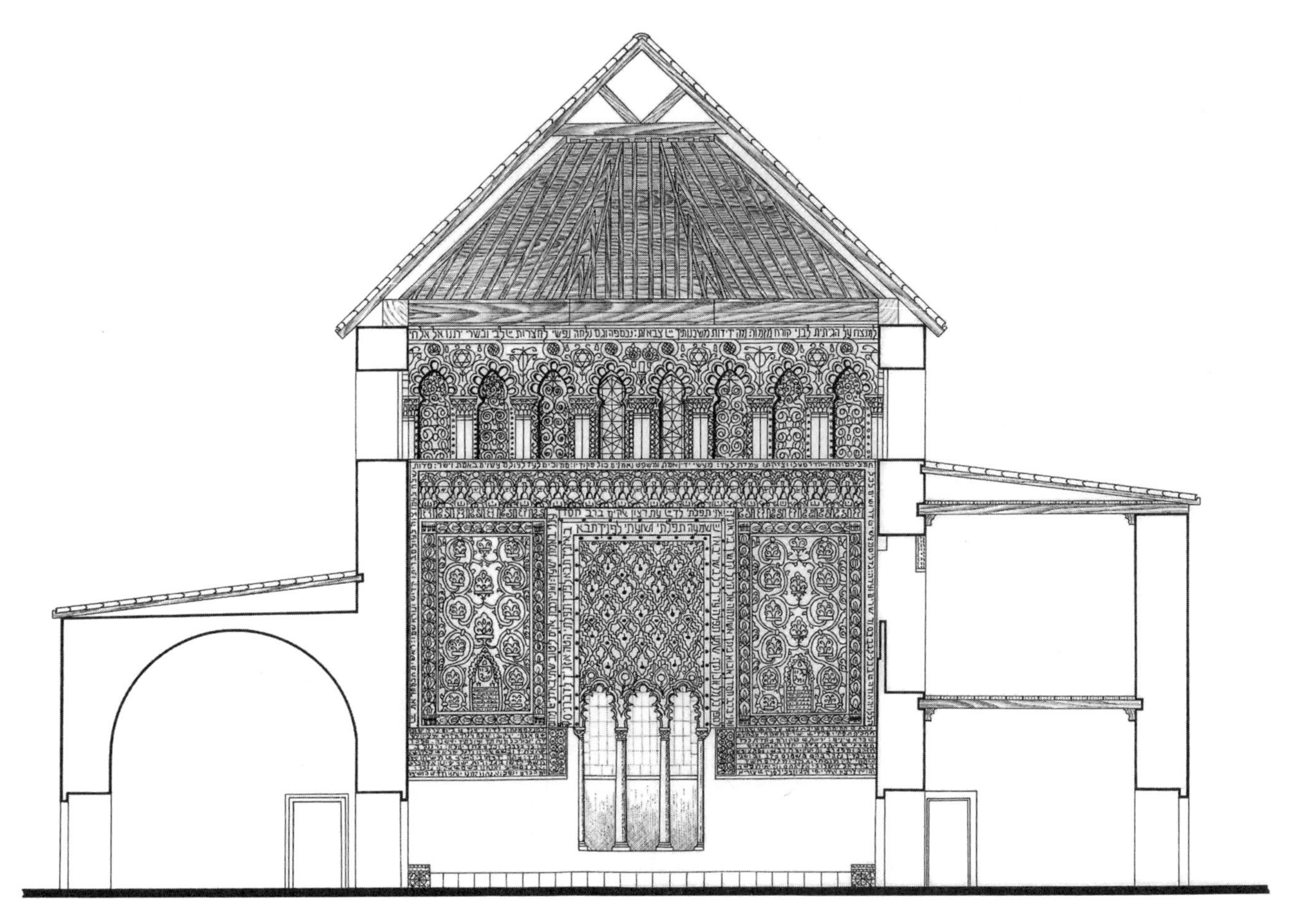

▲ Granada, the Alhambra, a view across to the snow-covered Sierra Nevada mountains.

▼ Granada, the Alhambra, a view toward the White Quarter in the city.

Granada, the Alhambra, the Myrtle Courtyard.

▲ Granada, Alhambra, the Lions Courtyard, in the middle is a fountain which according to tradition was seized from the home of the Abarbanel family.

▼ Toledo, view of the city from the outside. In front of it is the Tajo river and above it the Alcasar, the fortress.

Cordoba, the small synagogue, entry gate.